Cocker Spaniels

Joan Hustace Walker

BARRON'S

Acknowledgments

This book would not be possible without the generous help and expertise of the following amazing "Cocker" people: Gerry Foss, president of the Cocker Spaniel Rescue of New England; Vickie Dahlk, an officer of the Great Lakes American Cocker Spaniel Hunting Enthusiasts; and Veneé Gardner, owner of Gardian Cocker Spaniels.

About the Author

Joan Hustace Walker is a member of the Dog Writer's Association of America (DWAA) and The Authors Guild. The author of 18 books and hundreds of articles, Walker has been nominated for 27 national awards, and has received the DWAA's coveted Maxwell Award six times, including the award for the 2006 Best Single Breed Book. Joan has been active in conformation, obedience, performance events, and rescue at various levels of participation for the past 30+ years.

> All information and advice contained in this book has been reviewed by a veterinarian.

A Word About Pronouns

Many dog lovers feel that the pronoun "it" is not appropriate when referring to a pet that can be such a wonderful part of our lives. For this reason Cocker Spaniels are referred to as "she" in this book unless the topic specifically relates to male dogs. This by no means infers any preference, nor should it be taken as an indication that either sex is particularly problematic.

Cover Credits

Front cover and back cover: Shutterstock.

Photo Credits

Kent Akselsen: page 164; Cheryl A. Ertelt: pages 15, 16, 30, 69, 106, 146, 149, 152, 155, 156; Venee Gardner: pages 5, 163; Shirley Fernandez/Paulette Johnson: page 91; Curtis Hustace: pages 72, 171; Daniel Johnson: pages 83, 124 (top and bottom), 125 (top and bottom), 126 (top and bottom), 127 (top and bottom), 128 (top and bottom), 129 (top and bottom), 133 (top), 151; Paulette Johnson: pages vi, 12, 20, 22, 24, 37, 41, 43, 45, 46, 49, 51, 53, 55, 56, 60, 65, 66, 76, 81, 84, 86, 88, 90, 93, 98, 101, 102, 120, 133 (bottom), 137, 139, 140, 142, 143, 166, 174; Pets by Paulette: pages v, 3, 7, 8, 27, 32, 35, 39, 58, 79, 108, 130, 144, 178; Shutterstock: pages i, iii, 21, 59, 105, 158; Connie Summers/Paulette Johnson: pages 18, 113, 115, 117.

All inquiries should be addressed to:
Barron's Educational Series, Inc.
250 Wireless Boulevard
Hauppauge, New York 11788
www.barronseduc.com

ISBN-13: 978-0-7641-4413-4 (Book)
ISBN-10: 0-7641-4413-8 (Book)
ISBN-13: 978-0-7641-8678-3 (DVD)
ISBN-10: 0-7641-8678-7 (DVD)
ISBN-13: 978-0-7641-9709-3 (Package)
ISBN-10: 0-7641-9709-6 (Package)

Library of Congress Catalog Card No: 2009032995

Library of Congress Cataloging-in-Publication Data
Walker, Joan Hustace, 1962-
   Cocker spaniel / Joan Hustace Walker.
      p. cm. — (Barron's dog bibles)
   Includes index.
   ISBN-13: 978-0-7641-4413-4
   ISBN-10: 0-7641-4413-8
   ISBN-13: 978-0-7641-8678-3
   ISBN-10: 0-7641-8678-7
   1. Cocker spaniels. I. Title.
   SF429.C55W35 2010
   636.752'4—dc22   2009032995

Printed in China

9 8 7 6 5 4 3 2 1

CONTENTS

CONTENTS

The Cocker Spaniel has been the number one breed 25 times. That's more times than any other breed in the country. In addition, the Cocker has remained in the top-10 breeds for decades.

There's good reason for the Cocker Spaniel's long reign in popularity. She's a compact size, which makes her an easy fit in a wide range of homes. She is athletic and excels in numerous performance events, from agility and rally to formal obedience and flyball. The Cocker has also maintained her hunting instincts and can make an outstanding personal hunting companion on the weekends, and a loving family pet during the week.

Then there are the Cocker's good looks. Whether you prefer buff, red, black, roan, parti-color, or even sable, the Cocker Spaniel comes in a rainbow of colors and markings. Paired with a luxurious, full coat and those unmistakable dark, soulful eyes, the Cocker Spaniel is irresistible.

Of course, being one of the most popular breeds for so many years means that the Cocker Spaniel also has one of the longest-running problems with being unwanted dogs. Cocker Spaniel rescue organizations are filled to the brim with dogs waiting to be placed in new homes. Mostly, the Cocker finds herself homeless because her original owner wasn't prepared for the *real* Cocker.

So, if you're looking for a pet guide that will extol the virtues of the Cocker and convince you she is perfect for *you*, this isn't the book. This is the book that will give you the whole picture: the good, the great, the challenging, and maybe a few things that aren't as nice as they could be. Owning a Cocker can be an amazing experience, but if the match isn't right, a Cocker can be a very challenging dog to own. This book aims to make sure *the match is right!*

Have fun. If the Cocker Spaniel is the right dog for you, one thing is for sure: There will never be a dull moment in your home again. And, you'll never have to guess where your dog is; she will be at your feet . . . or under them, or in between them, or circling them . . .

Chapter One

All About the Cocker Spaniel

To many people, the Cocker Spaniel is the ultimate lap dog. Compact in size and sporting a luxurious coat, this precious dog with the dark, gentle eyes and sweet disposition makes for a wonderful companion. Underneath that charming exterior, however, centuries of hunting instincts and drives continue to course through this spaniel's blood, giving the Cocker a delightful depth of character not found in many pets.

Spaniel Origins

To fully appreciate and understand a Cocker Spaniel's behaviors, energy level, and overall temperament (not to mention conformation), it helps to take a look at the long history of the breed. It is believed that the Cocker Spaniel is a direct descendant of spaniels that were present in parts of the world hundreds, and perhaps even thousands, of years ago.

Of course, tracing the Cocker's history with any degree of certainty is difficult, if not impossible. Until the last century, the only information we had about spaniels was mostly gleaned from the hints given to us through art, sculptures, and early written records or historical references. Keeping detailed accounts of bloodlines, breedings, and even dogs' names is a relatively new phenomenon that occurred with the formation of the Kennel Club in England in 1873, followed by the American Kennel Club in 1884.

In fact, thousands of years ago, dogs were grouped by purpose. Dogs used for flushing out game from dense cover were called spaniels. It is from this generic spaniel that the Cocker is believed to be descended. There is some dispute, however, as to when the first mention of a "spaniel" was recorded and by what civilization.

Fun Facts

The spaniel is believed to have originated in Spain, as the origin of the word *spaniel* is credited to the Middle English *spaynel* or *spaniell*, or the Old French *espainnel*, an alteration of *espaignol*, meaning "Spaniard," or "Spanish Dog."

For example, a historian from the 1800s indicated that water spaniels were present in Roman times and that their likenesses appear on various monuments. Unfortunately, subsequent researchers were not able to verify these claims.

So, even though it is quite possible that the Romans employed a spaniel-type dog for hunting, the first written mention of a "spaniel" that has been verified occurs in Irish laws in 7 A.D. The laws noted that water spaniels were given to the king as a tribute.

Of course, these spaniels are specifically described as "water" spaniels, as opposed to simply "spaniels." This indicates that there was probably more than one type of spaniel present at the time, and possibly a division had already been made between the water and land spaniels.

Centuries later, references are made to there being two types of spaniels used for hunting: land spaniels for birds and small game found on land, and water spaniels for waterfowl. It is the land spaniel from which the Cocker Spaniel is believed to be descended.

Later still, mention is made of land spaniels being different sizes. Small hunting spaniels were ideally 14 to 20 pounds (6–9 kg), and larger spaniels were more than 28 pounds (12.5 kg). Additionally, a "toy"-sized spaniel emerged during the Middle Ages that was not used for hunting of any sort, and was strictly a darling of the court.

Land Spaniels

In 1328, Gaston de Foix, in the Anglo-Norman text *Livre de Chasse*, makes specific mention of a "spaniel" being used in the sport of hawking or falconry.

Foix describes spaniels as having come from Spain and being used when hunting with hawks. Additionally, Foix notes that spaniels could be used when hunting with nets and to retrieve birds that had fallen into water, as the spaniels could be taught to swim.

Additional descriptions of spaniels used in hawking occur in the *Boke of St. Albans*, a volume written in verse, which is usually dated as 1486. It is believed that this manuscript was written as a schoolbook and is largely a translation of *Le Art de Venerie*, written by Guillaume Twici (huntsman to Edward II), which includes much of the original *Livre de Chasse*.

Roughly a hundred years later in 1570, Queen Elizabeth's physician, Dr. Johannes Caius, wrote the *Treatise of English Dogges, their diversities, the names, the natures and the properties*. In this book, he gives a detailed description of the use of "Spaniells" in falconry and in netting. Evidently, the little spaniel's hawking and netting uses had not changed much in nearly 250 years!

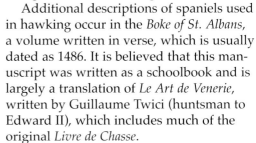

Breed Truths

Netting

Spaniels were used to flush game from cover and into nets. This method was used to capture not only partridges, quail, and pheasants, but rabbits and hares too.

Sweet Spaniels Thou Art

Insights into the loving, gentle nature of the spaniel occur nearly simultaneously with the first mentions of the spaniel's use in hawking and netting. It appears that the spaniel had her soft, fawning nature for hundreds of years. Though the spaniel was admired by many for her sensitive nature, other authors and poets used the spaniel as a metaphor for a willingness to bear untold beatings and hardships and continue to love someone who, in most cases, was rather undeserving.

An abbreviated history of the spaniel's appearance in some of the greatest works in English include the following highlights:

- In Geoffrey Chaucer's *Wife of Bathe's Prologue* (circa 1380), he pens this line: "For as a Spaynel she wol on him lepe."
- William Shakespeare makes multiple references to spaniels in several different plays, including *Julius Caesar, Macbeth,* and *King Lear* (circa 1595–1605). Perhaps one of the most quoted lines comes from *A Midsummer Night's Dream* in which Helena says to Demetrius:

  "I am your spaniel; and Demetrius,
  The more you beat me, I will fawn on you:
  Use me but as your spaniel, spurn me, strike me,
  Neglect me, lose me; only give me leave,
  Unworthy as I am, to follow you."

- In the early 1700s, famed Irish poet and author Jonathan Swift gives readers a glimpse into the conformation and spirit of the spaniel in his poem *On Rover: A Lady's Spaniel*:

  "Happiest of the spaniel race,
  Painter, with thy colours grace:
  Draw his forehead large and high,
  Draw his blue and humid eye;
  Draw his neck so smooth and round,
  Little neck with ribbons bound!
  And the muscly swelling breast,
  Where the Loves and Graces rest;
  And the spreading even back,
  Soft, and sleek, and glossy black;
  And the tail that gently twines,
  Like the tendrils of the vines;
  And the silky twisted hair,
  Shadowing thick the velvet ear;
  Velvet ears, which, hanging low,
  O'er the veiny temples flow."

- British poet William Cowper wrote a delightful poem in 1788, *Beau and the Water Lily,* that chronicles the loyalty

of a spaniel. According to the poem, the spaniel sees that his owner can't reach a water lily, so he swims out to pluck it himself and drops "the treasure at my feet."

> "Charmed with the sight, 'The world,' I cried,
> 'Shall hear of this thy deed:
> My dog shall mortify the pride
> Of man's superior breed.'"

The Spaniel as a Gundog

Written references to spaniels and the appearance of spaniel-type dogs in various forms of artwork continue through the 1600s and 1700s; however, it is not until the late 1700s and early 1800s that mention is made of a "cocking" spaniel.

At this point, it appears that two sizes of spaniel were in use in England. The smaller of the spaniels, the Cocker, is thought to have derived her name from her ability to hunt woodcock, a type of bird that is typically found in thickets and dense underbrush in England—rugged undergrowths that the larger spaniel had difficulties entering.

In John Ashton's book, *The Dawn of the XIXth Century in England,* the author describes "cock hunting with spaniels" as it was done in 1804. Ashton explains that the hunter used teams of two dogs.

In the early 1800s, the hunter had to be a good shot; Ashton notes, "When a covey rose, not a shot was wasted, if possible, for, by the time the gun was reloaded, the birds would be far off." A flintlock musket, roughly the same weapon that had been used since the late 1600s, would have taken up to 30 seconds to reload. The birds wouldn't be just gone; they would be in the next county!

One illustration in the book, labeled "Cock Shooting with Spaniels—1804," depicts two hunters with their muskets along with two parti-color (black-and-white) cocking spaniels (of the same size as today's Cocker Spaniels) dashing gaily about the hunters' feet. Another illustration shows three spaniels asleep at their owner's feet after a day of hunting. Ashton notes that the spaniels were the master's "constant companions," which is true of the breed even today.

Fun Facts

The Spaniel in Art

Spaniel-type dogs have appeared in art since the early 1400s. Two particularly famous pieces from this period include Antonio Pisani Pisanello's *St. George Rescuing the Princess of Trebizond* and *The Vision of St. Eustace.*

In the painting of St. George, a small, buff-colored spaniel-type dog is seen in the foreground. The dog is standing next to a Greyhound and is roughly the size of today's Cockers.

In the painting of St. Eustace, three types of dogs are visible: a Greyhound; two dogs that are primarily white with red markings and no apparent feathering (similar to a smooth pointer's coat); and, near the base of the painting, two spaniel-type dogs, with feathered coats and solid red in color.

How a Flushing Spaniel Works

Throughout the long history of the spaniel, and the more recent history of the cocking or Cocker Spaniel, the way in which the spaniel seeks and finds birds for the hunter has remained relatively the same for centuries.

Basically, the Cocker "quarters" the ground, in a busy, crisscrossing pattern. The Cocker hunts in areas where birds are normally found, such as in brushes or fence rows, using her scenting abilities to pick up traces of scent either in the air above the vegetation, or on the ground as a scent trail. As the Cocker sweeps back and forth in front of the hunter, she makes little noise, but her docked tail is held low and wags quickly. As the Cocker finds a scent trail and nears her quarry, the pace of her tail wag quickens until her entire body begins to wriggle ecstatically, lending to this dog her common description as a "merry little Cocker."

When the Cocker locates the birds, she pauses slightly and then dives into the cover to flush the birds into the air. Though retrieving was noted as a skill that the spaniel could be taught in the Middle Ages, at some point, asking a spaniel to retrieve fell out of style with hunters. In a hunting instruction manual written in 1814, the author clearly tells hunters that it is advisable to train their spaniels to find the fallen bird, but *not* to retrieve it: ". . . it is no part of my system to suffer a dog ever to

Breed Truths

In the early days of firearms, accuracy was not all that great and range was very limited. Therefore, a good hunting spaniel was "close working," and did not range too far from the hunter; otherwise the hunter could not hit his targets.

touch a bird: no! the generous triumph of a conscious *find dead* is all." The author continues with ". . . none of your poaching fetch-and-carry kind of business . . . I wish to take my game home handsome; in condition such as might render it acceptable to a friend."

However, as the range and accuracy of rifles improved, and the distance the hunter had to walk to pick up the shot birds increased substantially, it became more popular to add the "retrieve" to the very willing Cocker Spaniel's repertoire. By the late 1800s, the Cocker was not only expected to retrieve birds, but once again, expected to retrieve birds from water. The Cocker was not used to hunt waterfowl; however, she had to be proficient in retrieving game from ponds, lakes, and streams as well as on land. The Cocker did all of this with her usual enthusiasm and merriment.

The use of the Cocker was not limited to woodcocks, of course. The dog was also a popular choice for hunting other game birds that liked to hide in gnarly undergrowth, such as the pheasant, and was used to hunt small game, such as rabbit. And, according to some accounts, the Cocker was used in Greyhound coursing to flush out hares for the Greyhounds to chase.

Though popular in England as a hunting dog in the 1800s, the Cocker was not as widely appreciated in the United States. American author William Youatt wrote in his book, *The Dog* (published in 1857), this of the Cocker Spaniel: "This beautiful and interesting dog, so called for his peculiar suitableness for woodcock shooting, is but little known among us except as a boudoir companion for our ladies." Youatt went on to expound on the abilities of the little Cocker, should she be employed as a hunting dog in the United States: ". . . no doubt, if introduced into our country, [the Cocker Spaniel] would prove equally, if not more serviceable, in putting up game concealed in the thickets and marshy hollows of our uncleared grounds."

Youatt was correct in his predictions. Within just a few decades after his comments were published, the Cocker Spaniel became popular as a hunting dog in the United States as well.

The Formation of a Purebred

Though the name Cocker had been affixed to the smallest of the hunting spaniels since the late 1700s, and though a "type" was emerging that made the small spaniel look different from other spaniels, the Cocker as a distinct "breed" wasn't really established until the early 1900s.

Before this time, a land spaniel weighing less than 25 pounds (11.25 kg) was classified as a Cocker. If the dog weighed more than 25 pounds, she was a field spaniel. It was quite possible, therefore, for a dog to be exhibited at a dog show as a Cocker one year, and then as a field spaniel the next year.

Eventually, a shift began to take place in which fanciers pursued their interest in establishing the Cocker as a breed, as opposed to a weight

classification. In 1885, the Spaniel Club was formed in England with the goal of developing breed standards to distinguish the different types of spaniels by their hunting traits and conformation. In 1892, the Cocker was given "breed status" by the Kennel Club (United Kingdom), but it would be nearly another 10 years before the weight restrictions were removed as a defining trait between a Cocker and a field spaniel.

Cocker Spaniels Divided: English and American

Fun Facts

The first spaniel thought to come to America was a dog that came along with the Pilgrims on the *Mayflower* in 1620.

Around the time that England was working to better define the Cocker Spaniel as a breed, fanciers in America were working on the same project. In 1881, a group of wealthy Americans formed the American Cocker Spaniel Club, which later became the American Spaniel Club (ASC).

The first item on the club's agenda was to develop breed standards that would clearly define and separate Cocker Spaniels from field spaniels. The task turned out to be an arduous one, taking more than 20 years to complete. Finally, in 1905, the Cocker Spaniel had its own standard and its own studbook; no longer were field spaniels and Cockers considered the same breed, nor could they be interbred.

But, the Cocker was not finished in her evolution. Both England and the United States had developed breed standards for the Cocker Spaniel;

Fun Facts

In the early 1900s, one dog fancier lamented that women were purchasing Cockers based on the dog's coloring and how well they felt the colors would blend with their homes and clothing.

however, breeders in these countries had different ideas about how the ideal Cocker should appear as far as type, size, and coloring. The changes were subtle at first, but as time marched on, the American version of the Cocker Spaniel was markedly different from the English version.

In 1942, Ella B. Moffit, an American breeder of Cocker Spaniels, wrote in her book, *The Cocker Spaniel*, that she admired the "consistently good necks, shoulders and straight fronts" of the English-bred Cockers; however, she also says the English-bred Cockers have "plain heads, small eyes and houndlike muzzles . . . which make the English and American Cockers incompatible."

In 1946, the American Kennel Club recognized English Cocker Spaniels as a breed separate from Cocker Spaniels (the American type). England followed suit, and separated the two types as Cocker Spaniels and American Cocker Spaniels.

Pampered House Pet versus Hunting Dog

It appears that concerns about whether the popularity of the Cocker Spaniel as a pampered house pet could destroy the Cocker's innate hunting abilities are not new.

Moffit also relates in her book that in England during the Victorian era, the Cocker had become a "symbol of aristocracy" and "was to be found in every domicile which combined refinement with necessity for canine companionship." The same fate of a pampered house pet (as opposed to a dog that could hunt *and* be a house dog) appeared to be taking place in the United States as well, where Moffit notes that sportsmen "insultingly dubbed [the Cocker] as 'parlor pets'" and didn't recognize the Cocker as a sporting dog.

A resurgence in the popularity of hunting Cockers was initiated in 1923 by Moffit and she was able to prove her point: The Cocker could still hunt and retained many, if not most, of her natural flushing talents. The popularity of the Cocker as a hunting dog gathered momentum, but after several decades, the desire to hunt with a Cocker in the field began to wane again.

FYI: Presidential Pups

James Monroe's wife, Maria, had a pet spaniel during her husband's term (1817–1825). As it was a lady's pet, it is likely this spaniel was of the smaller, Cocker-type dog.

Rutherford B. Hayes (1877–1881) owned a small black-and-white spaniel named Duke that appears in photos to be a Cocker-type spaniel.

Harry S. Truman was reportedly given a beautiful, blonde Cocker Spaniel puppy as a gift in 1947. . . The pup was given to the White House physician, who in turn gave it away. The dog was passed on to several people until the pup wound up with a chief petty officer, who was given permission to take the Cocker with him to Italy, provided he never mentioned that the dog had belonged to Truman.

While serving as vice president, **Richard Nixon** owned a Cocker Spaniel, Checkers, who is credited with saving his political career in 1952 when Nixon mentioned Checkers in an emotional speech.

John F. Kennedy was given a black-and-white Cocker Spaniel in 1963 by the prime minister of Ireland.

With Cocker numbers dropping in field trials, the American Spaniel Club held what many believed at the time to be the last field trial for Cockers in 1962. Fortunately, Cocker owners who wanted to preserve the hunting tradition of their spaniels persevered.

In 1972, Working Dog tests were designed by the American Spaniel Club to evaluate the hunting ability of Cockers. In 1985, the American Kennel Club introduced an experimental program of "hunt tests." The noncompetitive events turned out to be wildly popular and the hunting Cocker began to reemerge. By the 1990s, Cockers were regularly earning hunt titles. Cockers were once again entering field trials, and in 2001, a Cocker Spaniel was awarded a field championship, making the Cocker's return to the field official.

The Darling of the Show Ring

Though interest in the Cocker Spaniel as a hunting dog has ebbed and flowed through the last century, the story of the Cocker's popularity in the show ring is quite different.

Helpful Hints

Which Cocker Is It?

Books written about Cocker Spaniels that predate 1946 refer to the Cocker Spaniel (the predecessor of both English and American varieties). To determine which kind of Cocker an author is referring to in books written after 1946, you will need to find out if the book was published in England or in the United States.

Famous Cockers

Who can forget these Cocker Spaniels that have been immortalized through books, movies, and advertising?

Spot—This little Cocker was made famous through the *Dick and Jane* beginning reading books.

The Coppertone puppy—The little black Cocker that is seen tugging at a little girl's bikini bottom was reportedly modeled after the artist's neighbor's dog.

Lady—Perhaps the most famous buff-colored Cocker Spaniel of all time, Lady is the perfect, beautiful dog in Disney's movie *Lady and the Tramp*.

In conformation events, the Cocker has one of the most enviable win records in the United States. At Westminster Kennel Club, the oldest and longest running show in the country, the Cocker has claimed 63 group placements and four Best in Show wins from 1877 to 2008.

There's no denying that the Cocker Spaniel has a lot of flash in the ring. With a coat that sweeps the floor on legs, and nearly to the floor on chest and sides, the Cocker Spaniel presents a colorful, fluid, eye-catching silhouette as she moves effortlessly around the ring. What's not to love about this dog?

The popularity of the dog in the show ring, however, has developed a Cocker that differs somewhat in type from the popular hunting dog of the 1920s through the 1950s. The biggest difference? The coat. Photos of Cockers from the late 1800s through the 1950s reveal a spaniel with *some* feathering or longer coat on the ears, legs, and "pants" (rear thighs) of the Cocker. Today's Cocker has such a profuse coat, in fact, that most pet owners keep their dogs in short clips.

The Effects of Popularity

The Cocker's winning presence at dog shows and her near celebrity status when owned by presidents, politicians, and famous actors and actresses is largely blamed for the breed's skyrocketing in popularity.

Unfortunately, going hand-in-hand with a long-running, number one status is almost always a corruption of temperament and health in a breed—no matter which breed holds the most popular spot. Demand for the Cocker as a household pet simply outstripped the ability of high-quality breeders to place dogs in homes.

The biggest loser in the popularity game was the Cocker Spaniel. In the 1950s and 1960s, unhealthy, ill-tempered Cocker Spaniels wound up in homes. As a result, the Cocker quickly gained a reputation of being a snippy, unhealthy dog that was unreliable with children.

Bred for centuries to have a sweet spaniel temperament, the Cocker Spaniel, which was also noted for her robust health, had been brought to a new low point in her history in just a matter of a few popular decades. It was a devastating blow that would take decades to overcome.

HOME BASICS
Decoding Cocker Colors

In the show ring, Cockers are judged in varieties, which are based on their coloring: black, parti-color, and Any Solid Color Other than Black (ASCOB).

The Cocker may be any of the following colors or combinations of colors:

Black	Buff	Red Roan
Black & Tan	Buff & White	Sable
Black & White	Red	Sable & White
Black, White & Tan	Red & White	
Brown	Silver	**Markings:**
Brown Roan	Blue Roan	Roan
Brown & Tan	Blue Roan & Tan	Ticked
Brown & White	Cream	White Markings
Brown, White & Tan	Golden	

Fortunately, high-quality breeders never lost sight or love for their breed. It is through these folks that the Cocker regained (and in many cases, never lost) her wonderful, consistent temperament and much of her good health.

The healthy, happy, *merry* little Cocker is still alive and well; however, potential owners need to make the effort to find a high-quality breeder who breeds for excellent conformation and impeccable temperament and tests his or her dogs for heritable diseases.

Into the Twenty-first Century and Beyond!

Today's Cocker Spaniel is truly a versatile breed. This merry little spaniel can do it all—compete as a show dog, earn hunting titles, perform in obedience and agility, serve as a valued therapy dog, *and* be possibly the best companion dog you'll ever own.

Loving, loyal, and eager to please, the Cocker Spaniel remains one of the most popular breeds because she is capable of filling so many owners' expectations of the perfect dog.

Fun Facts

Celebrity-Owned Cocker Spaniels

Kate Beckinsale	Lily
Elton John	Arthur and Marilyn
Naomi Watts	Ned
Oprah Winfrey	Sadie (Ivan, Sophie, and Solomon, deceased)
Barry Williams (a.k.a. Greg Brady of *The Brady Bunch*)	Buffy

Chapter Two

The Mind of the Cocker Spaniel

The Cocker Spaniel is renowned as being a merry little dog: a friend to all and foe to none. With a beautiful coat, expressive eyes, and a compact size, the Cocker seems to have it all. Of course, the Cocker Spaniel is much more than just another cute dog; her origins as a flushing spaniel give this breed more depth than first meets the eye.

The World According to the Cocker Spaniel

The Cocker Spaniel carries with her the genetics of hundreds of years of selective breeding for specific physical and mental traits. These traits *do* affect how a Cocker Spaniel sees her world, how she is likely to react to different situations, and how easy or difficult it is for her to adapt to varying types of lifestyles.

Of course, when looking at how the Cocker Spaniel might fare in the home, it is important to take into consideration *all* the purposes for which the Cocker has been bred and how these changing roles have influenced the behavior, health, and temperament of today's Cocker Spaniel. For the Cocker, this means that potential owners not only should be well-versed in the little spaniel's role as a hunting dog, but also understand how reigning as a winning show dog has influenced the further development of this breed.

A Sporting Dog First and Foremost

As a sporting breed that was developed specifically to locate, flush, and retrieve small birds, the Cocker Spaniel was bred to be a close-working, intelligent dog that learned new skills quickly and had an earnest desire to please her owner. Since flushing spaniels often worked in pairs, the hunting Cocker needed to be friendly with both people and dogs. And, of course, in order to search for birds in thick underbrush all day, the Cocker needed to have boundless energy and a solid work ethic (i.e., she didn't call it a day after she found her first woodcock, but kept working to find more).

Though it may have been generations since a puppy was actively bred for the field, the Cocker Spaniel still retains hunting characteristics in varying degrees. The traits that you are most likely to see in the home that relate to the breed's hunting background include a higher-than-average activity level; a nose that can sniff out fave toys and yummy treats no matter how well hidden they are; a strong desire to be with her master; and the need to be given a job, lest the "work" she will find to busy herself be viewed as destructive by her owner.

A Show Dog Extraordinaire

In the 1930s, the Cocker Spaniel hit the show ring with a bang. The breed was a regular winner in the Sporting Group ring. To gauge just how popular this little dog was—and continues to be—in the show ring, a look at the Westminster Kennel Club records (1921–2008) for all varieties of Cocker Spaniel indicate that a Cocker Spaniel won Best in Show four times and placed in the Sporting Group ring 63 times. To put these numbers in perspective, during the same relative time period (1923–2008) the Labrador Retriever had only eight group placements and no Best in Show wins.

The Cocker's extended popularity in the show ring brought with it efforts to refine the breed's look, which resulted in a more luxurious, flowing coat (as opposed to the sparser coats of early hunting Cockers), longer legs, a shorter back, and the distinctly American Cocker head type that is seen with today's dogs.

The Price of Popularity

With the breed's popularity in the show ring also came increased visibility among the public. When pet lovers discovered that the Cocker was a perfect house pet for many families, the dog fell subject to the same issue that has plagued every wildly popular breed through the last century: indiscriminant breeding.

Dishonest people seized the opportunity to prey on the public's wants, which outpaced the ability of reputable breeders to produce high-quality puppies. Puppy mills, puppy brokers, even the neighbor next door got involved in breeding Cocker Spaniels, all with no regard for hereditary diseases or temperament. As a result, the poorly bred Cocker Spaniel developed a reputation for serious health problems and temperament issues, a stigma that honorable breeders are still fighting today.

Fortunately, members of the American Spaniel Club became deeply concerned with the increasing numbers of health issues that were occurring

within the breed and invested heavily in research to determine causes, cures, and tests to prevent hereditary diseases. The continued efforts of breed club members to help develop a healthier Cocker have gone far in reducing the incidence of chronic and fatal hereditary diseases. In fact, because of these efforts, the Cocker Spaniel you will find today is a much healthier dog (when purchased from a reputable breeder) than she was decades ago.

However, not all hereditary diseases have been eradicated, and research for many diseases and chronic conditions that continue to affect the Cocker Spaniel is ongoing. If there is one big warning about purchasing a Cocker Spaniel puppy it is this: To assure that you are receiving a healthy dog that possesses the joyful, friendly temperament that really makes the Cocker Spaniel a top family choice, you must seek out a reputable breeder who tests for hereditary diseases, tracks his or her lines for disease, and makes sound, friendly temperaments a top priority.

Why the Cocker Spaniel Is a Great Dog

The Cocker Spaniel hasn't been the reigning "most popular dog" in the past century without good reason. The following are some of the breed's most well-loved traits that help to make this dog a terrific pet.

1. **Merry, playful temperament:** As a flushing spaniel, the Cocker's manner of hunting has been—and still is—described as "merry." The Cocker thoroughly enjoys being with her master and displays her joy with a full body wiggle that begins with her docked tail and works up through her entire body.

2. **Highly adaptable:** Because the Cocker was bred as a close-working hunting dog, she loves to be with her people. As long as the Cocker's needs are met (and that includes lots of companionship and sufficient exercise), the Cocker can adapt to living in most households, from city apartments to country estates.

3. **Small but sturdy:** The Cocker is the smallest of the sporting breeds; however, she is quite solid and less likely to get injured by an owner's misstep or a medium-sized dog's play than other small dogs her size.

4. **Luxurious coat:** Thanks to the show folks who worked to develop the Cocker's thick, profuse coat, this breed is great for those who love the look, touch, and feel of a long coat.

5. **Wide variety:** The Cocker Spaniel comes in an incredible array of colors and marking patterns. If you can't find a color or parti-color that you like with the Cocker, then the color may not be in existence.

6. **Intelligent:** As a dog that was originally bred as a hunting dog, the Cocker is a highly intelligent, enthusiastic pupil that is eager to learn new skills.

7. **Soft, sensitive temperament:** The Cocker Spaniel is so in tune with her owner that she picks up on subtle changes in voice and body movements easily, making her a joy to train using positive, reward-based methods.

8. **Athletic:** The Cocker's coordination, balance, and agility make the breed a fun choice for competing in a variety of performance events.

9. **Bonds to entire family:** Some breeds bond strongly to one family member and tolerate the others. Not the Cocker; this spaniel tends to enjoy the entire family's company.
10. **The Cocker *can* hunt:** Yes, those centuries-old traits are still present, and many more breeders are getting involved in working tests, hunt tests, and field trials, making this breed a truly all-purpose dog.

What's Challenging About the Cocker Spaniel?

Every breed has aspects about it that make raising a puppy and living with an adult dog in the home a challenge. Which aspects of the breed you will find challenging depends greatly on your lifestyle, your willingness to meet your dog's needs, and your expectations for your canine companion.

The following are some of the characteristics of the Cocker Spaniel that many Cocker owners find whimsical, endearing, or at the very least tolerable, and other owners may find frustrating:

1. **Soft, sensitive temperament:** The Cocker Spaniel is more sensitive to a stern look or a threatening tone of voice than many of the larger, thicker-skinned (temperament-wise) hunting dogs, such as the retrievers and pointers. Harsh words and physical corrections are not tolerated well by the Cocker, and repeated use often leads to the dog shutting down completely or developing other temperament issues. This is not a dog that can be manhandled.
2. **Extensive coat care:** Long, wavy, or curly coats mat and tangle easily. The Cocker's coat requires constant attention and a commitment to daily grooming. Cockers can be kept in one of several, less-maintenance-heavy clips, but grooming fees can be quite expensive (about $50 every six weeks).
3. **Shedding:** The Cocker is not a hypoallergenic breed; she *does* shed. Peak shedding times are spring and fall, and in temperate climates, year-round.
4. **Not an outdoor dog:** Though the Cocker loves to be outdoors, she is not an "outdoor" dog. The Cocker Spaniel will suffer mentally if she is kept in the backyard and not allowed to be with her family.
5. **Higher activity level:** With such a strong hunting background, the Cocker Spaniel has more energy than the average dog. Many owners mistakenly think that the Cocker doesn't require the level of exercise that bigger hunting dogs need and, as a result, don't exercise their Cockers enough. (Then these same owners can't figure out why their Cockers are ricocheting off the walls of their home and destroying everything in sight. Hmm . . .) Clue: The Cocker is a *spaniel*. She needs to stretch her legs on a daily basis!
6. **Shadow effect:** The Cocker Spaniel likes to follow her master from room to room. She likes to touch and be close. She so enjoys being

with her family that if she's not trained to be comfortable being alone, she can develop separation anxiety issues.

Breed Truths

The average life span of a Cocker Spaniel is 12 to 14 years. Males typically weigh 25 to 30 pounds (11.25–13.5 kg), females, 20 to 25 pounds (9–11.25 kg).

7. **Barking:** If the Cocker Spaniel is not getting enough exercise, mental stimulation, or attention, she may begin barking more than you'd like to get your attention.

8. **Smell:** The Cocker Spaniel must be groomed regularly to keep her coat clean and odor-free. In addition, painful ear infections and certain skin conditions can produce awful odors and require immediate veterinary attention; impacted anal sacs, or those that have expressed onto the coat, produce a horrendous smell too.

9. **Health disorders:** As noted previously, many inroads have been made over the past two decades in breeding for a much healthier Cocker Spaniel; however, the breed still has many chronic illnesses that can be difficult and expensive to treat, such as allergies, autoimmune diseases, and skin disorders. The puppy buyer is truly dependent on the breeder for health testing. Working with a reputable, experienced breeder is an absolute *must* with this breed.

10. **Temperament issues:** When a breed is so popular that everyone and their neighbor is breeding them, you're going to find quirky temperaments. *This is true of every breed that has held the number one mark for more than a few years.* With that said, the resilience of the Cocker Spaniel's true temperament has weathered the storm better than most, as is obvious by the wonderful Cockers that are in breed rescue, through no fault of their own. If you are purchasing a puppy, however, it is essential that you purchase a pup from a reputable, knowledgeable breeder who breeds for temperament and provides an enriching environment in which the pups can grow and flourish.

Cocker Spaniels as Family Dogs

The correct Cocker Spaniel is an excellent companion with people of all ages, from responsible, young children to elderly relatives living in the home. The Cocker is playful, a real cuddler, and up for anything anyone wants to do, whether that's playing a game of fetch (yes, many Cockers have a strong retrieving instinct that is quite intact!), going for a walk, or taking a car ride.

COMPATIBILITY Is a Cocker Spaniel the Best Breed for You?

	Rating
ACTIVITY LEVEL	● ● ● ●
AFFECTION	● ● ● ● ●
SENSITIVITY	● ● ● ● ●
EASE OF TRAINING	● ● ● ●
EASE OF HOUSETRAINING	● ● ●
FRIENDLINESS TOWARD OTHER PETS	● ● ● ●
FRIENDLINESS TOWARD CHILDREN**	● ● ●
WATCHDOG	● ● ●
GUARD DOG	●
COAT CARE (CLIPPED)	● ● ● ●
COAT CARE (FULL)	● ● ● ● ●
SHEDDING	● ● ● ●
HEALTH*	● ● ●
OK FOR BEGINNERS	● ● ● ● ●

1 to 2 dots = below average; 3 dots = average; 4 to 5 dots = above average

*Well-bred dogs will be above average health; others will be below average health.
**If socialized or raised with children.

Because of overbreeding (dating back to the late 1960s), the Cocker Spaniel earned a reputation for being a poor choice for families that carries over even today. The truth is that an outgoing, friendly Cocker puppy that is raised in a loving home and is given adequate, high-quality opportunities for socialization with people and dogs is going to be a terrific pet.

Of course, problems may arise even with a high-quality puppy *if* the Cocker is raised without any clear leadership or if she is raised in isolation and grows fearful of people. Friendly, well-adjusted, social Cocker Spaniels require training and socialization to help them reach their full potential as gregarious, well-adjusted adult dogs.

CAUTION

The number one cause of dog bites is *not* dominant aggressive dogs; rather, it is fearful dogs.

Unsocialized, poorly bred Cockers that are raised in a stressful environment (for example, confined to a crate in a barn or garage; living in crowded or isolated conditions; whelped by a fearful mother) are more likely to be fearful than the well-bred puppy that comes from a line of outstanding, friendly temperaments and is raised in the home by an experienced, hands-on breeder.

For this reason, it is critical for potential Cocker Spaniel owners to seek out an outstanding breeder *or* go to a good breed rescue, where the adult dog's behavior with children is known. If you are a parent, it behooves you to invest the time and effort into finding the most outgoing, "knows no strangers," highly tolerant, cuddly lover of a dog—or the puppy born with the greatest potential to become a wonderful family pet.

With Other Pets

The Cocker Spaniel was bred to work well with other dogs, and this trait is still seen today. When socialized with other species (such as the family cat) and provided with high-quality, positive play with other puppies and dogs growing up, the Cocker Spaniel is quite friendly with other animals. There are always exceptions to the rule, however, and often that occurs with fearful or socially inept dogs.

A fearful dog will often be leash aggressive, for example, because she is afraid of other dogs. While being walked, she knows she has nowhere to escape (she's on leash, after all), so she will often put on a big show to keep

the oncoming dog at a distance. Unsocialized dogs may actually be quite friendly toward other dogs, but if their body language is a bit rusty (from lack of interaction), what they mean to communicate to the other dogs may be a bit off or confusing.

Fearful dogs *can* be worked with, and strides can be made to improve their comfort level with other dogs and pets. Likewise, the social dinosaur can also brush up on her play moves and make a few friends (see page 00).

Cocker Spaniels and Learning

Cockers excel at learning. In studies performed in the 1950s and 1960s, Cocker Spaniels were found to excel at learning skills that required restraint, or waiting for the next command. A look at their history as flushing spaniels gives us the reason for this: Cockers that were successful in the field were required to show restraint after flushing birds out of their cover as the hunter shot the birds. In these same early, behavioral studies, however, Cockers were shown to be miserable in problem solving when it involved manipulating something with their paws or teeth.

Of course, these studies were performed more than half a century ago, before the Cocker drifted away from field events for more than 40 years. So, how is the Cocker today when it comes to learning?

The Cocker Spaniel continues to be a fun dog to train, particularly when using positive, reward-based training. She has retained her eagerness to learn and is commonly seen as an enthusiastic participant in performance events, including obedience, rally, agility, hunt tests, and tracking.

Cocker Spaniel First-Year Expenses

Routine Veterinary Care (healthy puppy)*	$200
Surgical (spay or neuter)	$150
Food*	$241
Grooming (every six weeks)	$450
Crate or carrier	$60
Exercise pen	$80
Kennel boarding (10 days)	$200
Training classes (12 weeks)	$250
Treats*	$68
Toys*	$45
Average First-Year Cost	**$1,744**

*Estimate from 2005–2006 APPMA National Pet Owners Survey; many pet owners will spend substantially more.

The only limiting factor when it comes to training Cockers, whether for performance events, housetraining, or simple house rules, is that this breed is and always has been a sensitive spaniel. She is not a dog that accepts rough handling. The greatest benefit of a sensitive dog, however, is that she accepts an owner's leadership easily through simple training exercises and is not a dog to challenge this leadership once it is established.

Putting It All Together

The true Cocker Spaniel is a joy to live with, and her enthusiasm and playfulness is contagious. She is a terrific family pet among respectful children and is remarkably adaptable to many different lifestyles as long as her needs are met. She is content to be a family pet, a competitive athlete, or an on-the-go companion perfect for the active adult.

If a pet owner wants to experience the *real* Cocker Spaniel, the Cocker Spaniel as she was intended to be, it pays both financially and emotionally to seek out the well-bred puppy or adopt a rescued Cocker who is old enough that her health issues (if she has any) are known.

Breed Needs

Children must be raised to treat the family pet with kindness. It's not fair to expect a dog not to react to pain from being poked in the eye, pinched, stabbed with a pencil, or tackled. For this reason, it is essential that parents commit to never leaving a toddler or young child (who doesn't know better) alone with a puppy or dog. Supervise or separate—and work on teaching your children how to handle the puppy or rescued adult dog with respect.

Chapter Three

How to Choose a Cocker Spaniel

ocker Spaniels are bred to be active, intelligent, loving, "soft"-tempered dogs of smaller size with long, soft coats. Within the breed, of course, there is a wide range of variation in not only how a Cocker may look but also in how she may behave. To choose the best Cocker Spaniel for your home, it's wise to be aware of all the variations that can occur in the breed.

Cocker Spaniel Choices

Most Cocker Spaniels are very active; this is a breed that is supposed to be able to work in the field all day and have bursts of high speed. There are some Cockers, however, that are so busy they *must* have a job, such as participating in hunting, obedience, agility, or flyball. A few Cockers are willing to melt into a sofa, but they are usually the exception, rather than the rule.

Besides varying activity levels, Cocker temperaments can run the gamut from the classic, gentle spaniel to those that are quite bold and pushy, and those who are timid with very little self-confidence.

Then there's the size range that can be seen in the Cocker. Cockers bred for the show ring are very uniform in height (males $14\frac{1}{2}$–$15\frac{1}{2}$ inches (36–39 cm); females $13\frac{1}{2}$ to $14\frac{1}{2}$ inches (34–36 cm) and weight 20 to 25 pounds (9–11.25 kg)). If a particular pup is going to grow up to be much smaller or larger than this range, a knowledgeable breeder will be able to tell you this when the pup is only eight weeks old. Puppies whelped by not-so-knowledgeable breeders are not nearly as uniform in size and can range from the very small (12 to 14 pounds/5–6 kg) to what is more commonly found, dogs weighing 30 pounds (13.5 kg) or more at maturity (and not overweight).

In addition to differences in size, you will also find that there are several different types of Cocker Spaniel coats. The correct coat is a swishy straight or slightly wavy coat; however, it is not unusual for a Cocker to have a thick, dense, curly coat. Some coats are silkier to the touch; others are almost cottony in texture. If you are keeping your Cocker trimmed in one of several pet clips, the type of coat your dog has may not be too important. If you plan to maintain a full coat on your Cocker, it is important to find a puppy or adult that has a correct coat, since it is easier to keep tangle-free than a cottony or densely curled coat.

In addition to coat types, there are also myriad coat colors, markings, and patterns that make every Cocker unique. Basically, Cockers are divided into three color varieties: black, ASCOB (any solid color other than black), and parti. Black includes not only solid black, but also black with tan points; ASCOB includes a range of solid colors, as well as brown with tan points; and parti includes not only dogs with two colors (a solid color and white), but also tri-colored dogs.

For more on color variations, see "Every Color of the Rainbow," page 29.

Narrowing Down the Choices

With so much variation within the breed, how do you choose a Cocker? Much of your selection will be based on personal preference and what you find most appealing in a dog. Careful consideration should be given to selecting the Cocker that has the greatest chance of succeeding in your home. Possibly the best place to start in considering what you want in the perfect Cocker is to determine whether raising a puppy or adopting an adult dog will best fit your lifestyle and goals for the Cocker.

Adult or Puppy?

It used to be that when shopping for a new dog, most people automatically thought "puppy." This is no longer the case, as dog owners are discovering that the "rescued" adult dog has an amazing amount of potential as a cherished companion.

Puppies

Puppies are adorable. Benefits of puppies are that they bond quickly with the entire family, and a puppy is often more easily accepted into a household with other pets, particularly if you have other species, such as cats.

There are other benefits to raising a Cocker Spaniel puppy too. With a puppy, you will be able to

- make sure your Cocker is well-socialized with all kinds of people;
- select a puppy that will have the greatest potential to excel in a specific activity or performance event, such as conformation, agility, or hunting;

- limit the risk of serious genetic illnesses by purchasing a puppy through a high-quality breeder who has his or her dogs health tested;
- acclimate your puppy to the demands of your lifestyle; and
- experience those precious few months of owning a puppy.

Adult Dogs

Thousands of Cockers are given up to Cocker Spaniel rescues every year. If you are interested in adopting, you'll be amazed at the range of colors, markings, ages, and personalities of the adoptable spaniels available in your area or region.

The advantages of adopting an adult Cocker are many, too. With an adult dog, you will be able to

- sleep through the night;
- keep your home intact, since the adult dog is past the chewing stage and tends to be a little less active;
- know what your Cocker's health problems are as an adult, because she is an adult;
- know the Cocker's true, adult character; and
- allow the dog to pick *you*. It's uncanny, but when an adult Cocker picks *her* humans, she is rarely ever wrong in making a lasting match.

In general, though puppies are very, very cute and adorable, raising a Cocker puppy is a huge undertaking. Housetraining doesn't happen overnight and requires diligence and work on the part of the owner. Pups also can't hold for longer than two to four hours and will require at least one potty break in the night.

The biggest potential disadvantage to purchasing a puppy is that most Cocker puppies that are readily for sale are not high-quality pups. Most of the puppy mills that have been halted in recent years *were breeding Cocker Spaniels.* The Cocker Spaniel also is a popular breed for backyard breeders to sell. For these reasons, it is absolutely *vital* that you work only with reputable, experienced, high-quality breeders. For more information on finding a high-quality breeder, see "Breeders," page 35.

One of the biggest advantages of adopting an adult dog is that what you see is what you get. There's no guessing about the size the Cocker will be when she's all grown up, or what type of coat she'll have after she sheds her soft puppy coat. And most important, you'll know exactly what her adult temperament is and have a good idea about any potential health problems she might have.

The rescued dog will still need training, and the adopter needs to understand that since the Cocker is *not* naturally a self-confident dog, it may take a little while for the rescued dog to be comfortable in her new surroundings and completely trusting of her new owners.

Male or Female?

With the Cocker Spaniel, there are relatively few differences between males and females. Males tend to be about an inch taller; there are females who are larger than average, however, and certainly some males that are more petite than normal.

Along with this slight size difference, female Cockers may have a slightly different, some say more feminine, appearance to their heads and overall expression. The difference in this "look" is very subtle, and as you might have guessed, there are refined-looking male Cockers, and females with stronger features.

In addition, the following are some sex-specific characteristics that should be considered when trying to decide between the sexes.

Males

If a Cocker Spaniel is intact, he will be distracted by females when they are in season. He may climb or dig under fences to get to his love interest. He may stop eating for days and complain pitifully for weeks. High levels of stress may cause increased shedding and/or matting in the dog's coat. Neutered dogs do not have any of these issues.

Another "intact" male issue is "marking" or urinating to mark territory. Many Cocker owners say they've never had a problem with intact males marking indoors; however, some owners have had different experiences. Housetraining and the use of belly bands may be necessary with male Cockers. Neutering before a year of age often prevents the problem of marking, but it's not a guarantee.

Females

Female Cockers are generally smaller than males, but of course, this isn't always the case. Female Cocker Spaniels will also come in season at least once or twice a year. During this time, *some* Cockers can become "moody," though other words have been used to describe the female dog's behavior during estrus. Moodiness aside, keeping a female Cocker's coat clean while she is in season can be problematic, even with doggie diapers and other such products. Along with the raging hormones comes another side effect: "blowing coat." Large amounts of coat may shed (and mat) because of the fluctuation of hormones.

Of course, a female Cocker that is spayed will not have any of the above issues, nor will she run the risk of an unwanted pregnancy.

CAUTION

If you are considering adopting a Cocker Spaniel from a local shelter or humane society (as opposed to a Cocker Shelter rescue), make sure that the Cocker has had a temperament evaluation by a qualified staff member or trainer.

Best Choice?

The final word on whether you should chose a male or a female Cocker is this: Don't put sex as your number one deciding factor. If you find the perfect Cocker in rescue (and he's a male), please consider him. If a top-notch breeder says she has the *perfect* Cocker puppy in her litter for your home—and the puppy is a female—don't discount her because you wanted a male. Get to know the Cocker puppy or adult as an individual and then make your choice.

Every Color of the Rainbow

Do you want a particular color or color pattern? The rule with color preferences is similar to that of considering boys versus girls: Keep an open mind. Ultimately, the color of a Cocker Spaniel is secondary to her temperament and health.

In general, coat color is a personal preference; however, there are some instances in which the color or the pattern of the color could affect the quality of the Cocker's breeding and health.

First, the basics: Cockers come in solid colors, solid with tan points, tricolor, and parti-color coats. Of the solid colors, the most popular color has

been buff for many, many years. Buff can range in intensity from very pale to very rich in color. Another popular color in the show ring (but not so much with pet owners) is black. Other solid colors include silver, gold, chocolate, and red.

Cockers with tan "points," markings that are similar to the tan markings of Rottweilers and Dobermans, have a base coat of either black or chocolate. A Cocker may be tri-color, too, with black, tan, and white markings (similar to Bernese Mountain Dogs) or chocolate, tan, and white markings.

Breed Truths

Color-Coded Temperaments?

Some people swear that buff-colored Cockers are most active, blacks are sweetest, and parti-colors are braniacs. This may be true among certain breeders' lines; however, overall, temperament is more a factor of a puppy's parents and her environment.

Parti-color Cockers, or "partis," are those that are a solid color (i.e., black, chocolate, red, buff, etc.) and white. For the show ring, the white must cover at least 10 percent but not more than 50 percent of the Cocker's body. The white areas may be clear of any markings or they may be ticked. Ticking is the presence of small spots or "freckles" of the primary color in the white portion of the Cocker's coat. Ticking is considered a marking pattern and is not a color per se.

Another marking pattern that can occur in the white portion of a parti-color

PERSONALITY POINTERS

Mirror, Mirror on the Wall, Who's the Sweetest of Them All?

Many people who are searching for the perfect Cocker think female dogs are the sweetest, cuddliest, and most endearing of the sexes. This is usually not the case. When it comes to Cockers, females tend to be slightly more independent, sometimes a little more protective (not a desirable trait in a spaniel), and perhaps a bit more likely to have their own agenda.

The male Cockers, on the other hand, tend to be very patient, loyal, and apt to crawl into your lap for a snuggle. Perhaps snuggliest of all are neutered male Cocker Spaniels: Without the need to search for eligible females, the neutered male Cocker is pretty much all about loving you.

Behaviorists conjecture that this subtle difference between the sexes is natural for most breeds: Females *need* to be a bit independent in order to whelp and provide for their puppies.

Cocker is called "roan." The roan pattern is the intermingling of the primary coat color (i.e., black, buff, red, chocolate) with the white hairs.

And then there's sable . . . A true sable is a dog that has black hairs intermingled with the primary coat color. A sable can be solid (for example, a red sable would have black hairs intermingled with a red coat) or a parti-color (for example, a chocolate-and-white sable would have black hairs intermingling with the chocolate portion of the coat).

Though a Cocker can be registered with the AKC as a "sable," it is not possible at this time to compete in conformation at AKC dog shows. Sables can be exceptionally striking, and if one catches your fancy, it is perfectly fine to purchase a sable from a *reputable* breeder or adopt one from a rescue.

Beware the "Merle"

Merle is a coat pattern in which patches of the dog's solid color are diluted or faded. For example, a black dog with a merle pattern will appear to have spots of black on a gray coat. Merles often have blue eyes too. Though the merle markings are quite pretty, this coat pattern is not accepted by the American Spaniel Club.

The merle coat pattern has the misfortune to be linked with serious health problems. In particular, when two merles are bred with each other, the puppies are more likely to be blind, deaf, die shortly after birth, or have significant defects, such as the absence of eyes. And, that's in addition to all the other potential health problems that a Cocker can inherit.

FYI: The Genetics of Coat Color

Did you know that a jet black, solid-colored Cocker Spaniel may be a homozygous black (carrying only genes for black, with all resulting puppies black), or a heterozygous black (carrying recessive genes for colors other than black)?

If you find the genetics of coat color fascinating, check out the following:

- *www.vetgen.com/canine-coat-color.html* is an Internet primer on the genetics of coat color.
- *Futuredog: Breeding for Genetic Soundness* by Patricia J. Wilkie (Minnesota Extension Service, 1999)
- "A review of the genes affecting coat color and pattern in domestic dogs" is an article written by S. M. Schmutz and T. G. Berryere that was published in 2007 in the journal, *Animal Genetics* (volume 38: pages 539–549).

Theories abound about how the merle gene was introduced into Cocker Spaniels, as this marking pattern is believed to have occurred only in the past 25 years. Some fanciers conjecture that it is a genetic mutation. Others have traced the emergence of this coat pattern to one particular Cocker. Still others feel that the merle markings were originally caused by "one that got over the fence" and are indicative of an accidental breeding with another breed.

Regardless of how the genetics for this marking pattern were introduced, the majority of merle Cocker Spaniels are sold at high prices by breeders who are pitching these Cockers as being incredibly special for their rare color. Ufortunately, anyone who breeds specifically *for* the merle coat pattern is not a reputable or responsible breeder. At any rate, a merle Cocker Spaniel *is not worth more money*. A merle Cocker is strictly pet quality.

Breed Truths

Obo

The Cocker Spaniel that is considered the founding father of the breed was a beautiful, solid black Cocker Spaniel named Obo, bred by James Farrow (of England) in 1879. Obo's father, Frank, was black and tan; his mother, Betty, was black and white.

If your heart is set on a certain color or a specific marking pattern, be patient in finding your puppy or adult Cocker. Do not be tempted to go to a breeder with questionable breeding practices to find the color Cocker you want *now*. In fact, though you might have a color preference, it's always best to find a puppy or adult with a fantastic temperament and good health. Color and markings are really secondary when trying to find a perfect family pet or companion.

Show and Field Lines

With many of the sporting breeds, there is a distinct difference between dogs that are bred to succeed in the show ring and those that are bred to be personal hunting dogs or to compete in field trials and hunt tests. Often "field-bred" dogs differ in conformation or "build" from their show dog counterparts, and possess higher energy levels, and extremely strong drives to find birds.

Fun Facts

The first Cocker Spaniel to win Best in Show at Westminster Kennel Club was Ch. Midkiff Seduction, a black-and-white parti-color with black ticking in her white coat.

With the Cocker Spaniel, there is not a big difference between Cockers bred for field and Cockers bred for show. In fact, most people who are interested in hunting their Cockers go to the top show kennels to purchase their dogs. (This is true, too, of people who want to compete in agility, obedience, rally, flyball, and other canine sports.)

Though the interest in hunting Cocker Spaniels has fluctuated over the past century, the Cocker did not lose her ability to hunt. In fact, at a recent National Specialty show held by the American Spaniel Club, participants were invited to instinct-test their Cockers for hunting drives and abilities. Owners, handlers, and breeders brought their show dogs, agility dogs, and rescues to be tested. Of the nearly 50 dogs tested, all but two passed.

What this means, of course, is that in addition to having the instincts to hunt, most well-bred puppies will also have the accompanying drives and characteristics of a hunting dog: more specifically, a higher activity level, the need for mental stimulation, a keen interest in finding birds, a desire to work, and an intense need to be with their humans at all times.

FYI: What's Up with Sables?

Sable Cocker Spaniels are recognized as a legitimate color by the Canadian Kennel Club and the United Kennel Club. The current breed standard written by the American Spaniel Club (ASC) does not allow sables to be shown in American Kennel Club (AKC) dog shows. What is controversial is that sables *were previously* allowed entry in AKC shows for roughly a century, with multiple sables earning championships.

In the 1980s, several efforts to include wording that would make sable allowable in ASCOB and parti-color varieties were unsuccessful. A majority of ASC members voted "for" adding sable, but not enough members voted to constitute the two-thirds necessary for a change in the breed standard's wording.

There are Cocker breeders who continue to breed high-quality sable Cockers, exhibiting their dogs in Canada and in UKC dog shows, with the continued hopes that they will be allowed in AKC shows in the future.

Backyard Cockers

So, though field and show lines are largely interchangeable, the one line that is distinct and very different from show and field dogs is the backyard-bred or puppy mill Cocker. These are Cockers that are not bred to better the breed, but solely to produce puppies and an income.

The problem with dogs from less-than-reputable breeders is threefold.

Helpful Hints

Less Is Better?

The early Cocker had a much sparser coat, and was less likely to get hung up on brambles and branches than today's full-coated Cocker. Those interested in hunting with their dogs simply keep the heavy show coats clipped short for working in the field.

- First, backyard and puppy mill breeders do not test for hereditary diseases. The hereditary diseases that plague the Cocker Spaniel are chronic at best and fatal at worst.
- Second, these breeders do not screen for temperament. Often sketchy dogs are bred with each other simply because they are an eye-catching color or are fertile. Temperaments are a product of both genetics and environment. The pup that is born to a terrified mother is going to learn at an early age to be terrified herself.
- And third, backyard and puppy mill breeders do not breed "to standard," or to the ideal Cocker Spaniel conformation and type. In other words, this puppy may or may not look like a purebred.

Finding a High-Quality Breeder

To find a *good* Cocker Spaniel, you must find a high-quality breeder. There is no other way around this. The bad news is that there are more disreputable breeders than reputable breeders selling Cockers. The good news is that if you know where to look, it's easy to find a high-quality breeder.

Breeder Referral

The American Spaniel Club, regional Cocker Spaniel clubs, and local all-breed dog clubs have "breeder referral" systems in place to help puppy buyers find good breeders in their area. Call or e-mail the designated breeder referral person to get in contact with a breeder in your area. (See "Resources," page 167, for listings.) A recommended breeder may not have a litter of puppies *at the moment*; however, he or she will be able to refer you to another good breeder who does.

Breed Truths

Well-bred Cocker Spaniel puppies do not cost more than ill-bred pups, particularly in the long run. The potential for serious health problems in this breed is so great that a well-bred puppy may save you *thousands* of dollars in veterinary care and a lot of heartache over the years.

Dog Shows

Several magazines, such as the *AKC Gazette*, *Dog World*, and *Dog News* publish information about upcoming dog shows

FYI: Titles Explained

The success of a Cocker Spaniel in the show ring, hunt fields, and agility ring are forever recorded with a title. Titles are a source of great pride for the Cocker's breeder, and most reputable breeders keep scrupulous records—not only for their dogs but on their dogs' progeny as well. The following are some of the most common titles seen with dogs competing in AKC events.

Before the Cocker's name:

CH	Champion (AKC)
FC	Field Champion (Field Trial)
AFC	Amateur Field Champion (Cocker handled by an amateur in Field Trials)

After the Cocker's name:

WD	Working Dog (a certificate awarded by ASC for basic flushing skills)
WDX	Working Dog Excellent (more advanced skill test, ASC)
JH	Junior Hunter (entry level, AKC hunt tests)
SH	Senior Hunter (mid-level, AKC hunt tests)
MH	Master Hunter (advanced level, AKC hunt tests)
CD	Companion Dog (entry level obedience, AKC)
CDX	Companion Dog Excellent (mid-level obedience, AKC)
UD	Utility Dog (advanced level obedience, AKC)
NA	Novice Agility (entry level agility, AKC)
OA	Open Agility (mid-level agility, AKC)
AX	Agility Excellent (advanced level agility, AKC)

that can be searched by date. Online, you can check with *www.akc.com* or *www.infodog.com/showcalendar* for dog show listings and ring times.

When at a dog show, be sure to purchase a catalog, which will list the breeder and owner information for each dog entered. Often, Cocker Spaniels are exhibited by professional handlers, so the handler may not be the dog's owner. The handler, however, can tell you everything you need to know about the Cocker and put you in contact with the dog's breeder or owner.

Performance Events

Cocker Spaniels excel at numerous performance events, and high-quality breeders (or their puppies) can often be found competing at local obedience, agility, and rally events. Sometimes these events are listed in the local paper, but more likely you'll need to search the same websites as for dog shows (see above). Talk to owners of dogs at these events and get their input about who they purchased their Cockers from and who they would recommend.

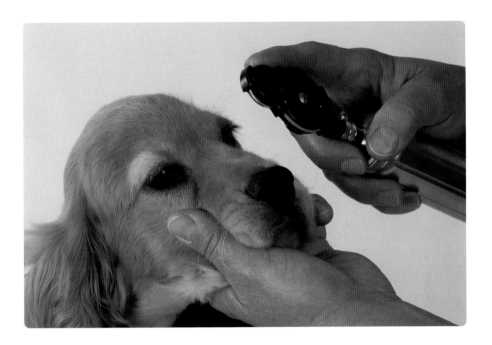

Health Screenings and Tests

The minimum recommended health tests for the Cocker Spaniel are hip dysplasia (certified free of disease by OFA, or PennHIP); and hereditary eye diseases, including retinal dysplasia, hereditary cataracts, progressive retinal atrophy, Dry Eye Syndrome, and primary glaucoma (certified free of disease annually by the Canine Eye Registry Foundation [CERF]).

Cockers that have been certified free of disease by OFA and CERF can be assigned a CHIC number from the Canine Health Information Center. This number assures that the Cocker's tests are current, and that the Cocker has a permanent form of identification.

Breeders, however, should be tracking far more than just hips and eyes. The following disorders are all believed to have a genetic link, and should be tracked not only in a breeder's dogs, but in their dogs' progeny:

Allergies Though a definite genetic link has not been found yet, researchers and breeders believe there is a hereditary

Breed Truths

A sign of a good breeder is that he or she will want to know everything possible about you (i.e., what your "dog" experience is, where you live, how much time you have for the new puppy, etc.), as well as making sure you know every-thing—good and bad—about the Cocker Spaniel. A great breeder is one who is available for every ques-tion you have, regardless of how stupid you might think it is.

37

factor to many of the more serious allergies found in the Cocker Spaniel. Cockers should be tracked for both atopic allergies and food allergies.

Autoimmune disorders Cockers have a predisposition for AIHA (autoimmune hemolytic anemia), in which the dog's immune system attacks her own blood cells, and autoimmune thyroiditis, in which the Cocker's antibodies attack substances in her body needed to form thyroid hormones.

Deafness Suspected dogs should be examined with a brain-stem auditory evoked response (BAER) test.

Distichiasis, ectropion, and entropion Distichiasis is a condition in which eyelid hairs grow oddly and may scratch the cornea. Ectropion is an excessive droopiness of the eyelids that may predispose a Cocker to eye infections. And entropion is a condition in which the Cocker's eyelids pull toward the eye, causing irritation and corneal scratches.

Epilepsy Idiopathic epilepsy is not uncommon in the Cocker. Breeders should be tracking progeny for this disease, and affected dogs should not be bred.

Heart Cockers can suffer from dilative cardiomyopathy and sick sinus syndrome. Cockers should be tested and registered clear of heart disease through the OFA.

Hypothyroidism Cockers frequently suffer from this condition, in which their bodies cannot make enough thyroid hormones. This condition is very treatable and dogs can be tested for it; however, those with the disease should not be bred.

Intervertebral disc disease With this disease, the disc between two vertebrae herniates or ruptures, pushing on the spinal cord.

Liver disease Chronic inflammation of the liver and copper toxicosis are two conditions that may be related and are becoming more prevalent in the Cocker. Tracking these diseases is important, as they may have a genetic basis.

Patellar luxation Also called a "slipped stifle," this condition is common in the Cocker. Dogs should be examined and certified free of this condition and registered with OFA.

Skin disorders Many of the Cocker's skin disorders (including seborrhea, a condition that causes the skin to become greasy, scaly, and odorous) are believed to have a genetic link.

Choosing the Puppy

If you've done your work and found a terrific, experienced Cocker Spaniel breeder, choosing a puppy becomes that much easier—mainly because the reputable breeder will know Cockers so well that he or she will be able to pick out the best puppy *for* you.

If you're not working with a breeder who is as experienced and have a whole litter from which to choose, the following are some tips to help you select a healthy, happy pup.

1. **Bring an expert with you.** If you're not sure what to look for in a puppy, it pays to hire an animal behaviorist, experienced handler, veterinarian, or trainer to come with you to evaluate the puppies for health and temperament.

2. **Are the puppies' parents happy, outgoing, and healthy?** The best possible way to gauge the future health, temperaments, and conformation of a litter of pups is to look at the parents.

3. **Visit the puppies several times, if possible.** Depending on when you visit with the puppies (i.e., just after they've eaten, right after a long nap, etc.), the puppies may behave differently. Try to see the pups when they're playing hard, as well as when they're all tuckered out.

4. **Watch how the puppies interact with each other.** If you want to know how a puppy is going to treat you and your family, observe how she plays with littermates. If she bites too hard and the other puppy yelps, does she change her play or does she continue to bully the other puppy? You want the puppy that plays nicely and understands doggie rules of conduct.

5. **Who wants to go home with you?** If you have a choice, the puppy that chooses you can be a successful match. When you walk away from the puppies, do any follow you?

6. **Avoid the shy, timid puppy.** Cocker Spaniels are gentle souls by nature and do not exude self-confidence. Though you don't want a bully (see No. 4), working with a shy or timid Cocker Spaniel can be very difficult and is often wrought with problems. A better choice is a friendly, outgoing puppy.

PERSONALITY POINTERS
Puppy Aptitude Testing

It would be nice if every puppy could be given a standard test, and from this test we could gauge the pup's potential temperament as an adult. The only problem is that there is no such thing as a perfect puppy test; however, the following tests may give you some further insights into how easy or challenging your Cocker will be to train.

Test	How to Test	What You Want to See
Boldness	While the pups aren't looking or are distracted, place an open box in their exercise pen.	What you'd like to see is curiosity without fear. Some Cocker pups may see the box as a great new toy and bound over; others may be a little more cautious. What you don't want to see is excessive or prolonged shyness (tail down, creeping toward box, or refusing to check out box).
Trust	Gently interlock your fingers underneath the puppy's tummy and just barely lift her off the floor. Hold for two to three seconds.	Cockers should be trusting by nature, so you want the puppy to be comfortable with this little lift. You don't want the puppy to panic and struggle the moment her paws lift off the floor. You also don't want her to try to bite you so you'll put her back down.
Reactivity	Stand several yards away from the pups and smack two blocks of wood together to make a loud (but not too loud) sound.	Watch to see how the puppies react. It's okay for the pups to be startled, but what you're looking for is what the puppies do *next*. Curiosity is great; returning to play as if nothing happened is good. You don't want to see a puppy frightened or hiding.
Retrieving	Toss a ball to each of the puppies.	Cockers have a lot of energy. If a Cocker enjoys a good game of fetch, it's one more way to interact with your dog and take the edge off of her energy supply. What you want to see is the pup run after the ball and pick it up. Bringing it back to you is an added bonus.
Companion Potential	Sit on the floor and call the puppy over to you.	What you'd like to see is a Cocker Spaniel puppy running over and bouncing into your lap. Kisses are always good too.

Adopting the Adult Cocker Spaniel

There's always good and bad news. The bad news is that popular breeds have huge rescue problems. Thousands of Cocker Spaniels are given up from adoption or rescued from puppy mills every year.

The good news? With so many good Cockers needing homes, you'll find Cocker Spaniels available for adoption in all different colors, ages, sizes, and personalities.

Rescues, Shelters, and Other Facilities Compared

You will find Cocker Spaniels available for adoption at a wide range of facilities. Some organizations will be able to offer you a lot of help in choosing a Cocker Spaniel, and others are far more limited.

Cocker Spaniel Rescue This is the cream of the crop for finding a great adult Cocker. These rescues are run by experienced Cocker Spaniel owners, breeders, and trainers who work hard to place the right Cocker in the perfect home. The dogs are spayed or neutered; up-to-date on vaccinations; evaluated for health and possible chronic diseases by an experienced veterinarian; treated for any diseases and/or conditions; cleaned and fully groomed; living in a home with a "foster parent"; learning basic obedience commands; housetrained (or in the process of learning); crate trained (or learning); and thoroughly temperament-tested and evaluated for their acceptance of (or reactiveness to) other dogs, cats, kids, men, and small children.

Shelters Not-for-profit shelters can range from being amazing facilities that offer myriad services (comprehensive animal clinics, evaluations by expert animal behaviorists, experienced help and counseling in choosing the right dog, post-adoption training classes, boarding, etc.), to crowded facilities that are doing their best to provide shelter for unwanted animals on a shoe-string budget. Some shelters are no-kill (which often become full and have to turn away animals), whereas others euthanize unadoptable dogs to make room for new dogs as they come in.

Municipally Run Animal Control Centers Often called "pounds," these municipal centers are primarily designed for housing strays that are picked up off the streets, as well as dogs that have been relinquished by their owners. Dogs are treated for fleas and ticks, and provided with food and water, but often not much else is done. The dogs are kept in kennels, sometimes in group runs, and frequently have a limited time to be adopted before they are scheduled for euthanasia.

Helpful Hints

The American Spaniel Club maintains a list of affiliated rescues that are searchable by state on their website at the following address: *www. asc-cockerspaniel.org/index.php/ rescue/rescue-groups.html*. A Google search using "Cocker Spaniel Rescue" and your state will produce contact information too.

The Adoption Process

If you are adopting a Cocker from an animal control center, the process is relatively simple. You must be 21 years old to adopt a dog. Additionally, you must be able to show proof of residence and pay the adoption fee. No screening is done as far as your ability to care for the adopted dog, and no services are provided to evaluate the Cocker's temperament or health.

At a nonprofit shelter, in addition to the above requirements, you will fill out a questionnaire, which will ask more information about you, where you live, what your experience with dogs is, how your previous dogs died, who lives with you, their ages, and other pertinent questions.

Once you've completed the questionnaire, you'll usually be allowed to see all the dogs that are available for adoption. If you're interested in one in particular, an assistant will bring the dog out of the kennel or run and allow you to visit with the dog in a private room or play yard. If you think you've found "the" Cocker Spaniel, you can usually put a 24-hour hold on the dog and return the next day with family members to make sure the dog is a hit with the whole family.

When a match has been made, there's more paperwork to fill out and then you're free to take the Cocker Spaniel home with you.

With a Cocker Spaniel rescue, you will go through all the steps that you would have gone through at a nonprofit shelter, but in addition, the rescue will want you to come out and meet some rescue dogs or a volunteer will bring a couple of dogs to your home for you to meet.

In addition, most rescues require a home inspection (to make sure the information on your questionnaire is truthful), and once a dog is placed in a home, the rescue will check on you and the dog to make sure the transition has been a smooth one.

What to Expect

If the adult Cocker comes from a shelter or pound, living in a home may be a completely new experience. Cockers that are adopted from Cocker Spaniel rescue will have lived in a foster home; however, your home will be new.

Take life slowly. Don't push the Cocker Spaniel. Let her adjust to your home and your family on her own schedule. Watch for signs of stress and know how to respond (see Chapter 5, "Living with a Cocker Spaniel"). When she trusts you, she will look to you for confidence when experiencing new things.

Enjoy. Earning the love and trust of a rescued adult Cocker Spaniel is an amazing experience.

10 Questions to Ask a Breeder

The following are the top 10 questions you should ask a Cocker breeder, to make sure that you are working with one of high quality.

1 What breed clubs do you belong to?

Correct answer: The American Spaniel Club, the American Spaniel Club Foundation (health organization), and/or a regional Cocker Spaniel club, a local all-breed dog club, or a Cocker hunt club. Membership in these organizations shows a dedication to the breed and an effort to breed healthier Cocker Spaniels.

Incorrect answer: Does not belong to any club.

2 Are you active in the show ring?

Correct answer: Yes. This shows that the breeder is involved in improving the breed, and breeds "to standard." Bonus points: The breeder is also active in performance events, such as agility or hunt tests.

Incorrect answer: No involvement, breeds Cockers only to sell puppies.

3 Are you involved in Cocker Spaniel Rescue?

Correct answer: Yes. Breeder is involved either physically or financially or both. Additionally, the breeder takes back and rehomes any of the dogs he or she has bred regardless of the age of the Cocker or the reasons given by the owner.

Incorrect answer: No. Breeder feels unwanted Cockers are not his or her problem.

4 Have you had any health issues that you've had to work with to eliminate in your lines?

Correct answer: Yes. Statistically, every dog has the potential to pass along a genetic disease to his or her progeny. The conscientious breeder knows this and constantly works to keep his or her lines as free of disease as possible.

Incorrect answer: Denies that he or she has ever had any problems in his or her lines.

5 Do you health-test your Cocker Spaniels?

Correct answer: Yes. (See "Health Screenings and Tests," page 37.)

Incorrect answer: No. Denies the need or claims his or her lines are clear of disease.

6 Do you track the health of the puppies you've sold?

Correct answer: Yes. The breeder tries to stay in contact with all puppy owners and requests health updates and test results at certain intervals.

Incorrect answer: No. Or may claim to track the pups' health but has no records to show.

7 May I have referrals to other people to whom you have sold puppies?

Correct answer: Yes. Bonus points: Contact information for puppy owners whose Cocker Spaniels are now two or three years old and would know if their dogs have temperament issues or health problems.

Incorrect answer: No. Or provides outdated or incorrect contact information (and refuses to provide additional contacts or updated information).

8. May I come to visit with you and meet your dogs?

Correct answer: Yes. In fact, with a responsible breeder, it is likely that you'll never have the opportunity to ask this question; the breeder will ask you to his or her home first. The breeder will want to be able to meet *you* in person, so he or she can see how you interact with the Cockers and help to determine what puppy might be best for you.

Incorrect answer: No. Or, the breeder may make an offer to meet somewhere other than the breeder's home. Red flag: The breeder says there's no need to visit because he or she will ship anywhere and accepts credit cards.

9. Do you have any puppies available now?

Correct answer: Yes or no. Many of the best breeders are very selective in their breedings and may have a litter only once a year or once every couple of years. Even if he or she has a litter, often the puppies are reserved in advance, so none may be available. If this is the case, the breeder will be able to refer you to someone who might have puppies or may be taking reservations for an upcoming litter.

Incorrect answer: Yes. If a breeder is interested solely in making money, he or she will breed several litters a year and may have multiple brood bitches (all of which will be untitled—no champions on-site). There will always be puppies available or available soon.

10. Do you breed any other types of dogs?

Correct answer: No or a qualified yes. Most high-quality breeders will work with only one breed; however, on occasion, a breeder may have a second breed. All dogs are actively being shown or retired (successfully), and the dogs are all kept as house dogs.

Incorrect answer: Yes. Even worse? The person sells multiple breeds of dogs and/or sells mixes with the Cocker Spaniel, such as a Cockapoo (Cocker-Poodle cross).

Chapter Four

Caring for a New Cocker Spaniel

It's almost time for your new puppy or rescued adult Cocker to come home with you. Be forewarned that this breed is known for inquisitiveness and ability to get themselves into trouble. So, before your Cocker finds ways to entertain herself that you don't find quite so amusing, take the time now to ensure that your home is safe, inside and out.

Cocker-Proofing Inside and Outside

Most pet owners are able to troubleshoot the things in their homes and yards that obviously have the potential to be dangerous. It's the unexpected issues that usually catch even seasoned dog owners off guard. Here are some ideas on where to look for hidden dangers in and out of the home.

Indoors

The obvious preventive measure here is to keep all items up and off the floor. Young Cockers are quite oral and enjoy putting anything and everything in their mouths. It's part of the way they explore their world. They touch, taste, smell, and chew on items of interest.

What isn't so obvious is what items Cockers might find interesting to put in their mouths and just how dangerous these items can be.

Kitchen

With hard, easy-to-clean floors, the kitchen is often "command central" when it comes to caring for a new Cocker. Unfortunately, it's also the room that contains most of the dangers in the home.

Problems Cleaning supplies are often stored under sinks and contain caustic chemicals that can be fatal if swallowed. Scouring pads, sponges, and washcloths may be hung on cabinet hooks or stored in drawers and can present choking hazards. Certain foods, such as chocolate, coffee beans, onions, and garlic, which are often kept on low-lying shelves or in food drawers, are toxic and can be fatal if ingested in sufficient quantities (which isn't much for a little puppy). Garbage that is kept in a receptacle in the kitchen (even if it has a lid on it) can be knocked over and eaten. The contents of your kitchen garbage can cause serious diarrhea, vomiting, an acute case of pancreatitis, or death.

Solutions Put drawer and cabinet safety locks on all kitchen cabinetry that can be reached by a Cocker (usually up to counter height is fine). Take food off open shelves and place it behind locked cabinet doors. Keep your garbage can behind a closed door, in a safety-locked cabinet.

Helpful Hints

Safety locks are sold at many stores selling baby supplies and in the baby aisles of grocery stores; these plastic locks require some assembly, but when installed, they ensure that a cabinet or drawer can't be opened more than a finger's width unless a person flips the lock with his or her fingertip. (Fingers work on these locks; paws not so much.)

Bathrooms

If everyone in the family could remember to shut the door after every use, the bathroom wouldn't prove to be a hazard to your Cocker. But, even if your intentions are good, it's wise to safety-proof your bathrooms too.

Problems Trash cans are easily accessible and often contain tempting used paper products, such as tissues, facial cleansing wipes, cotton balls, cotton swabs, and feminine hygiene products. At best, if the Cocker attempts to eat these products, the items will pass. At worst, the Cocker may choke, or if the items actually make it into the gastrointestinal tract, they could cause a fatal blockage.

Other bathroom dangers include cleaning supplies that are stored under the sink cabinet, and, soaps, shampoos, razors, and sponges kept by the tub or shower. And finally, many over-the-counter medications and prescriptions are fatal (even one pill) if ingested by a Cocker Spaniel.

Solutions Store bathroom trash behind a closed cabinet door or invest in a heavy, high-quality lidded can (those with a foot press to raise the lid work well). Also, be sure to store cleaning supplies in cabinets with a kid-proof safety lock. Toiletries that are normally kept around the tub or in an accessible shower should be stored on a counter, out of reach of the Cocker. With medications, take *great* caution when taking out a dose. If you drop a pill, do not leave the bathroom until you've found it!

Home Office

In this day and age of technology, many people have a room or a portion of a room dedicated to work, complete with computers, printers, and supplies. Since there's no question that no matter where you are in your home, your Cocker will want to be with you, it's wise to Cocker-proof this room as well.

Problems Computers, printers, phones, televisions, monitors, lamps—these items all need power sources, which typically results in wires running everywhere in a room. Puppies *love* to chew on wires and cords, which can

result in horrible burns, shocks, and even death. Paper clips, staples, and other small items frequently fall on the floor. Your Cocker is likely to find these items before your weekly vacuuming; ingesting them can result in serious injury.

Solutions Gather cords, wires, and cables and safely contain them in guide strips specifically made to group cords and wires and keep them off the floor. With small office supplies, make sure that if you drop something, you pick it up immediately. Also, use a lidded trash can in your office.

Living Areas

Even though you feel as if you're keeping a constant eye on your Cocker Spaniel, there will be moments when she can find ways to get into trouble.

CAUTION

Craft rooms are often littered with tiny pieces of a variety of materials. Set up your room so that you can safely dispose of all debris, and consider putting a crate for your Cocker in this room. She can be with you but out of harm's way.

Problems Cords, wire, and power cables are problems in most living areas, including bedrooms. Knick-knacks that used to be safe on end tables and low lying dressers may look edible or chewable to your Cocker. And, probably the biggest issues in these rooms are things that are casually left "out." These items include TV remotes, jewelry, socks, cell phones, coins, toys (plastic action heroes and fashion models are apparently the most desirable), magazines, books, shoes, slippers, and the list goes on. Any and all of these items can present choking hazards to the Cocker.

Solutions Keep all cords and cables out of reach, or protected with a cable/cord guide that is impermeable to chewing. Clear knickknacks from tables and put them behind cabinet doors or on high shelves. Keep bedroom doors closed, and constantly patrol the couches, beds, and floors for loose items.

Outdoors

If you don't already have a fenced-in backyard, bite the bullet, spend the money, and fence your yard. A young puppy will usually stay close by; however, as soon as she gains a little confidence, she'll be off. It's also important to fence in your yard so that other critters and not-so-friendly dogs don't come onto your property and harm your Cocker.

If you currently have a fence, inspect it for any potential dangers. Make sure chain-link fences are intact, with no gaps between the fencing and the ground. With wood fences, check for loose or missing boards, and rotted areas near the ground that could break away (and provide an escape). Also, ensure that no nails are protruding from the fence. The Cocker Spaniel's large, protruding eyes are more easily injured than other breeds'.

Helpful Hints

Is It Poisonous?

Your pup has just devoured a decorative plant. Or, you dropped your prescription on the floor and your rescued adult Cocker just swallowed it. What now? If your Cocker has ingested a potential toxin, *call your veterinarian immediately*. Depending on what was ingested, you may be asked to induce vomiting, or your veterinarian may want your Cocker at the veterinary hospital STAT.

If the Cocker ingests the potential toxin after hours, call the ASPCA's Animal Poison Control Center at 1 (888) 426-4435. The ASPCA staffs this service 24/7 with qualified professionals who can tell you if the ingested item is toxic, as well as what action you need to take. (A $60 consultation fee may be charged to a credit card.) The Animal Poison Control Center also maintains a list of toxic plants at *www.aspca.org/pet-care/ poison-control/*.

Other Problems Many backyards contain poisonous to moderately toxic plants that are either growing wild or are part of planned landscaping. Some yards may contain water hazards, such as sunken hot tubs, pools, or a koi pond. Houses with raised foundations have crawl spaces that not only are a potential home to dangerous snakes and spiders but are also just big enough for a dog to access and difficult for a person to retrieve a pup or a frightened adult dog.

Solutions Remove toxic plants, bushes, and trees from your backyard or prevent your Cocker from having access to anything she might try to chew or eat with garden fencing. Use fencing to block water hazards, as well as safety coverings that will bear the weight of a dog without sinking into the water. If you have a pool, teach your Cocker to use the steps to exit the pool. Also, consider using a collar alarm device: When the device becomes completely wet, an alarm sounds in the home to let you know that your dog is in the pool or pond. To prevent a puppy or adult dog from running under the house or deck, attach sturdy lattice around all openings and check regularly to make sure it is intact.

The First Day

Everyone wants to see the new puppy! If at all possible, however, the first few days your new Cocker Spaniel is home should be quiet and all about *you*. It is important that your Cocker bonds to you and feels at home as quickly as possible. One of the first signs that she is bonding to you is her reaction to something new. Does she look back at you to see your reaction? If so, she is turning to you for guidance.

What you do when she turns to look back at you is very important: You should be calm, low-key, and nonchalant. If you react by saying, "Oh! What is that?" your pup's wariness toward the strange object, noise, or person will be confirmed. Instead of having a friendly conversation with your puppy, you have just told your puppy that she *should* be afraid! When your Cocker turns to you, be prepared to portray confidence and no fear in both your body language and your voice. Your Cocker will follow your lead. This is how she learned from her mother, and now she'll learn from you.

Once your Cocker Spaniel is comfortable in your home, and with you and your immediate family members, you can consider inviting other people over to your home and making calm, quiet introductions. Remember, it's the quality—not the quantity—of meetings with people that are critical to your Cocker's

BE PREPARED! Cocker Spaniel Supplies

During the first year with your Cocker Spaniel, you are sure to accumulate many different toys and grooming supplies; however, the following are some of the basic items that you should have on hand before your Cocker comes home with you.

Food Find out what food your breeder (or the Cocker rescue) has been feeding your Cocker Spaniel, and purchase the same food. You may switch foods later, if you'd like; however, doing so now will cause gastrointestinal upset. Loose stools or diarrhea not only seriously hampers your housetraining efforts (and is a mess), but may mask a serious, underlying disease or condition that needs immediate attention.

Bowls Stainless steel bowls for food and water clean up easily and don't break when you drop them. Look for bowls that are made for long-eared breeds; they look more cone-shaped (wider at the bottom and narrower at the top).

Snood This is a thin, stretchy socklike tube that can be pulled over the dog's head and keeps her ears out of the way of her food and water bowls. A snood is worn only when the dog is eating to keep debris out of those beautiful, long ears.

Collar A flat buckle collar or a quick-snap adjustable collar are good choices for either puppies or adult dogs.

Leash When purchasing a leash for a young puppy, choose a thin, lightweight leash so there's no big clip that might clobber her in the head when you're walking her. As she gets older, you can choose a sturdier leash, if you'd like. A 6-foot (1.8 m) leash is good for walks; a 4-foot (1.2 m) leash is often preferred for training. Avoid retractable leashes until you've trained your Cocker to walk nicely on a standard-length leash.

Crate When you can't keep your eye on your Cocker, she should be in her crate—at least until she learns house rules and is reliably housetrained. Dogs and people have their preferences as to what type: plastic two-piece crates or folding wire crates. Plastic crates are less expensive and easily cleaned. Wire crates have greater air circulation.

Bedding If you've adopted an adult dog and you know she's good with soft, fluffy bedding, you can purchase a nice mat for her crate, as well as a dog bed for when she's out of her crate. For puppies, it is often wise to start with a pee pad at the bottom of the crate and shred lots of newspapers to provide some softness and warmth. Ingesting bed fluff or swallowing bits of towel, as many busy Cocker pups are apt to do, can cause intestinal blockages.

Toys There's no such thing as too many toys! Five or six small or puppy-sized toys are good for a puppy; the same number but in adult size (labeled for a medium dog/chewer) will be appreciated by the adopted adult. More than six toys? Rotate the toys on a daily basis, so there's always a "new" toy in the mix to amuse your Cocker.

Housetraining Supplies It's not a question of *if* you'll need these supplies, but rather *when*. Good items to keep on hand include pee pads or newspapers, a good stain and odor cleaner made for urine and feces cleanup, and paper towels.

success in becoming well-socialized and comfortable with people. (For more tips on socializing your Cocker, see page 72.)

Puppy's First Night

Maybe you've had a long drive to bring your puppy home. Or, perhaps you've had your Cocker puppy most of the day and everyone is tired and ready to go to sleep. Or, so you think . . .

The first night in a strange home can be tough on even the bravest of Cocker Spaniel puppies. Your puppy is used to sleeping with five or more littermates. She's used to hearing other little heartbeats and staying warm in a puppy pile.

Your puppy is also used to her mother's comforting presence. Even when they're weaned and eating puppy food with their littermates, the puppies still have the near constant companionship of their mother.

And, your Cocker Spaniel pup is used to the nighttime sounds, sights, and smells of her former home. This includes the day-to-day routine of her breeder and her breeder's family, as well as the people who commonly go in and out of the breeder's home.

Breed Truths

The adopted Cocker will become a very loyal companion. The first few days she is home, however, it is critical that she be allowed to play only in a securely fenced yard. She does not realize that this is "home" yet, and if let loose in an unfenced area, she may try to escape to return to her former foster home, or simply escape because she's anxious about her new surroundings. Give her a chance to bond, and give her a safe, fenced yard.

PERSONALITY POINTERS
Your Rescued Adult Cocker

Your first day and night with a rescued adult Cocker Spaniel will be nearly identical to that of a puppy; however, it is even more important for you to keep these first few days, and even weeks, as low-key and stress-free as possible. Adult dogs often take longer to adjust to a new home than a young puppy. Whereas puppies react to fearful sounds, people, and things by scooting away, hitting the deck, or showing excessively "friendly" behaviors, the adult dog *may* react with fear biting. Until your rescued dog has acclimated to your home and is comfortable with her new surroundings (and has bonded with you), go slowly with your Cocker. Keep commotion to a minimum and allow her to settle into her new home at her own pace. Require her to follow the house rules, but do so in a positive, nonconfrontational manner.

Your home is all new to her. You are new to her. And, for the first time in your puppy's life, she is all alone. She is likely to cry. What do you do now?

In the not-so-distant past, pet owners were told to put their pups in crates and let them cry. This is very similar to the archaic advice that was given to new mothers (i.e., let your baby cry herself to sleep). Now both human and dog experts agree that this is not always good advice.

With puppies, there is a reason for the pup's crying. She could be cold. She could be hungry. She could have to relieve herself. She could be lonely. As the pup's new "parent," it is up to you to determine why she is crying, and help her.

CAUTION

Adult dogs coming from Cocker rescue organizations often haven't had much experience being carefree, fun-loving puppies. Don't be surprised if your adopted Cocker suddenly goes through a "puppy" phase, during which she chews and plays with reckless abandon.

- **If she's cold**—Give her extra bedding to snuggle down into. Cover her crate with a warm blanket so she has less space to heat with her body. Make sure her crate is not in a draft. Wrap a hot water bottle in a blanket and place it in her crate to help keep her warm. (Avoid electric heating pads, as the pup could chew through the electric heating elements and shock herself. These pads may also get too warm and burn the puppy.)
- **If she's hungry**—On her first day home, your puppy may have missed a meal, or even two, with the stress of adjusting to a new environment.

Or, your puppy may have eaten well, but with all the extra excitement of the day, her metabolism may be on a higher setting and she may require more food. If she hasn't eaten during the day, try warming her food a little bit in the microwave. This will increase the aroma and heighten the taste of the food, enticing even a finicky eater to dine.

Helpful Hints

Between eight and ten weeks of age, puppies go through a fear imprinting period, during which bad or frightening experiences can have a lifelong effect. For this reason, some breeders will recommend keeping the puppy at home during this time; other breeders will not release their puppies until they are past this imprinting stage.

- **If she has to relieve herself**—Your puppy will be more stressed than she has probably ever been in her life on her first day in your home. This holds true for even the happiest, most outgoing Cocker puppy, too, as lots of play and meeting new family members is fun but also stressful. Higher levels of activity and stress cause the metabolism to work at a heightened rate. The result? Food and water will work their way through the puppy's system more quickly, which means your puppy will have to urinate and defecate much more frequently than normal. If a new puppy is crying, the first thing to check is if she has to relieve herself.

- **She could be lonely**—If you've covered all the bases and determined your Cocker is not crying because she's cold, hungry, or has to relieve herself, then she is lonely. Resist the temptation to put her in bed with

you (you will wind up with a wet spot in your bed by morning because she's not housetrained yet), but do put her close to you. Her crate should be in your bedroom, and if you're okay with lying on the floor for a night or two, make yourself a comfortable spot and stay close to her. You are not coddling her; you are showing her that she can trust you to take care of her.

Your new puppy's adjustment to your home should take only a matter of days, if that. As soon as your puppy is comfortable at night, she will be quiet too.

CAUTION

A puppy or adult Cocker may be too anxious to eat her first few meals; however, that's normal. What is *not* normal is if your Cocker Spaniel is vomiting, has dry heaves, has diarrhea with or without the presence of blood, or is listless. These symptoms could be indicative of very serious and perhaps life-threatening disease. Your Cocker requires immediate veterinary attention. Do not delay taking your Cocker to your veterinarian or an emergency clinic.

Acclimating to the Crate

Crates are a good tool to use for more than just housetraining. A Cocker that is comfortable spending time in a crate has a place of refuge, a place to relax, a place that is the dog's and only the dog's. In addition, you can safely

BE PREPARED! Different Crates for Different Cockers

Crate Type	Advantages	Disadvantages	Best for:
Plastic crate	Inexpensive; lightweight; some types are approved for airline travel; more "denlike"; breaks down into two pieces (top and bottom); easy to wipe down or clean	Less airflow than wire crates; bulky to carry and store	The Cocker that likes an enclosed feeling; a less confident Cocker that needs an area of retreat
Wire crate	Excellent airflow and visibility from all areas of the crate; collapsible crates take up less space when folded	Heavy and more expensive; not approved for air travel; more difficult to clean	Confident Cockers that like to see everything that's going on; car travel when there's more restricted airflow in the car
Soft-sided Carrier	Lightweight; easy to carry; handy for carrying a puppy; approved for in-cabin airline travel; stylish	Too small for most adult Cockers; cannot be used for "crating," as the puppy can chew through the fabric sides; heavy to carry heavier puppies	Young puppies up to 20 pounds (9 kg)
Tentlike plastic piping and screen crates	Good ventilation while providing some shade; lightweight; easily folded and stored	Only for supervised crating, as the puppy or adult dog can easily rip through the screening	The calm Cocker attending an outdoor activity or other event requiring crating

contain your Cocker Spaniel when you can't watch her every minute. For the crate to be *safe*, however, your Cocker Spaniel must be comfortable in it and content to sleep and relax there, as opposed to trying to scratch and claw her way out.

Crate Tips

To acclimate your puppy or adult Cocker Spaniel to a crate, follow these tips to help make it a home.

Choose the best crate for your Cocker The crate needs to fit. The crate should be big enough for the puppy or dog to completely stand up, turn around, and lie down (all sprawled out, not just curled up). In addition,

the crate should be the type that the Cocker prefers: a plastic crate if she likes cozy spots; a wire crate if she wants to see everything going on around her.

Make it comfy Layer the bottom with a pee pad and mound shredded paper in the crate so that she can fluff her bedding. Some pads made to fit crates are soft yet virtually indestructible. If she's an adult or an older puppy that is past the chewing/ripping/shredding stages, you can put a soft, cozy bed in the crate. Encourage her to nap in her crate.

Keep it in a strategic place Your Cocker Spaniel will want to be where you are. Place the crate where you will be spending the most time and where she will be able to see the movements of the family. This is often the kitchen; however, be prepared to move the crate to various rooms where you will be during the day—or set up more than one crate in the home.

Allow free access Keep the door open so your Cocker Spaniel can go into her crate anytime she wants. If you have children, set down the law *now* that no one except the dog is allowed in the crate, and when the dog is in the crate, she is to be left alone. Period. Cockers need a quiet retreat in busy homes.

Make the crate inviting Associate positive experiences with the crate as often as possible. Toss treats into the crate. Feed your Cocker in her crate. Offer her a dental treat, a yummy chew, or an interactive toy to play with while she's in her crate. Also, if you have a plastic crate and your Cocker is reluctant to go into it, take the top off. Once she's comfortable lying down in her bed in the open crate, reintroduce the top of the crate.

Identification Options

If your Cocker Spaniel does not have a form of identification, odds are greatly against ever finding her should she be lost or stolen. Fortunately, there are several ways you can identify your Cocker with both temporary and permanent forms of identification.

Tags

A dog tag with the Cocker's name and your cell phone number with area code (because a dog can get lost anywhere) is the most easily readable form of identification, and it's the least expensive. The first thing a Good Samaritan looks for is a tag on a dog's collar. The only drawbacks to dog tags are that they wear down and become illegible. You'll need to replace your dog's tags every year or so. Additionally, the dog tag is attached to the collar with a small loop that can break or pull off if enough pressure is applied. Tags *do* pull off, leaving the dog with no form of identification. That's why it is advisable to have not only a dog tag, but at least one permanent means of identification too.

Tattoos

The puppy or adult dog must be anesthetized for the tattooing procedure. Many owners choose to have the Cocker's registration number tattooed on the dog's ear flap or inner thigh when the puppy or dog is being spayed or neutered, or getting her teeth cleaned. A drawback to tattooing a densely coated breed, such as the Cocker, is that when the hair grows back on the inner thigh, the tattoo is not clearly legible. In fact, it may not be visible at all. The presence of a tattoo is helpful, however, if the person who finds the dog knows to look in this area (most Cocker rescues look for this; a shelter may not), or if you think you've found your Cocker and need to identify her.

Microchips

A microchip is roughly the size of a grain of rice. It is implanted with a needle between the puppy or dog's shoulder blades. The procedure causes momentary pain, but the microchip doesn't appear to cause dogs any lasting discomfort. Once implanted, the information that you provide for a national registry is maintained for the life of your dog. This information can be accessed by anyone with a microchip scanner. Most veterinarians, animal control facilities, Cocker rescues, and shelters have a microchip scanner. When the chip is scanned, the national registry calls you with information on where your Cocker Spaniel is. Be sure to always keep your contact information updated.

Housetraining Made Easy

The Cocker Spaniel is an intelligent dog that wants to please her master. She is also a clean dog. So, housetraining is usually very easy, if you just follow a few rules.

Space

Puppies are born with a natural instinct not to soil the den or nursing area. As soon as they can wobble on their legs, they will move away from the puppy pile to relieve themselves. Before this time, the puppies' mother diligently cleans each puppy herself. The dog's innate urge to keep the bedding and eating area clean continues through adulthood. It is this canine characteristic that makes it possible for us to train our dogs to relieve themselves only in certain areas of the home.

With a puppy, keep the initial area small. Crates are often used because the puppy cannot relieve herself anywhere in the crate without soiling herself, so she will hold her urges and vocalize when she needs to be let out. Crates work well *if you never allow the pup to urinate or defecate in the crate.* If a puppy is forced to stand in a soiled crate, she can develop "dirty dog syndrome," in which the adult dog doesn't seem to care if she is living in filth.

If you are gone for several hours during the day, you might consider using an exercise pen to housetrain your Cocker Spaniel puppy. In the exercise pen, put a just-right-sized crate for the puppy to sleep in, a water bowl, and a few safe toys, and then cover the entire space with pee pads. Your puppy will choose a place to relieve herself in the exercise pen. When she's chosen a spot, you can begin picking up the pee pads in other areas—*gradually*. As she grows, to give her more room you can fasten a second exercise pen but keep the preferred pee pad in its place. Whenever you are home, however, encourage her to relieve herself outside by taking her out regularly, supervising carefully, and praising her when she relieves herself.

Helpful Hints

Typical signs of a Cocker looking for a place to relieve herself:

- A sudden stop in play
- Sniffing
- Circling
- Running behind furniture or disappearing to another room

Frequency

The Cockers that are housetrained the most quickly are those that have owners who never allow the Cocker the opportunity to make a mistake. To set your puppy (or adult dog) up for housetraining success, it's critical to never ask your Cocker to "hold" longer than she is physically comfortable. During *active*, daytime hours, a young puppy's limit is no more than two hours. For a four-to five-month-old puppy, this can be as long as four hours. For an adult Cocker, the limit is usually six hours. At night, a sleeping, young puppy may be able to last as long as six hours without requiring a nighttime bathroom break; an older puppy or adult dog can generally sleep the entire eight hours without problems.

Submissive Urination

Cocker Spaniel puppies commonly urinate when stressed. The puppy may cringe slightly (and urinate) or may completely flop over on her back (and urinate). This is a highly submissive behavior. Whatever you do, *don't yell at her*. She is urinating because she is frightened. Don't coddle or try to comfort her, either; this will only reinforce (in her mind) that she *should* be afraid. Instead, work to help her build up her confidence: easy obedience skills, agility, and games of tug (where you let her win) are all things that can help her. Also, consider clicker training (see page 111) to mark *good* behaviors (when she is confident and relaxed) and reward them.

Excited Urination

Young Cocker puppies also may urinate when they are exceptionally excited. Because Cocker puppies seem to be excited all the time, you may find your puppy is "leaking" a lot. Usually, as the puppy gains more control over her bladder (around four to five months of age), this excited urination starts to disappear. If it doesn't, or if it is accompanied by other symptoms, have your Cocker examined by your veterinarian. There could be a biological reason for the urination, such as a urinary tract infection.

Close Supervision

Even if your Cocker has just relieved herself, it is quite possible that she may have to urinate or defecate again rather quickly. Drinking lots of water, a burst of high-speed play, eating supper, after being crated . . . these are all activities that can cause a pup to have an urgent need to urinate or defecate *again*.

When your puppy or adult dog is outside of her crate or exercise pen, watch her closely! If she shows any of the classic signs of needing to relieve herself, take her outside immediately.

Praise

Cockers like to hear that they've been good dogs. When your puppy or adult dog relieves herself in the correct location, praise her quietly. What a good dog! Never punish her for relieving herself in the wrong place, unless you catch her *in the act*. Then you can say "Ah-ah!" (ideally just enough to stop the flow), and *gently* scoop her up. Take her outside, where you can praise her when she finishes up.

On Command

Did you know you can teach your Cocker to relieve herself *on command*? When she is about to relieve herself, say "Go potty!" (or words of your choosing). Reward her with praise when she has finished. Soon, she will connect the words (*Go potty*) with the action. This command is exceptionally helpful late at night (when you want to go to bed and your Cocker wants to sniff around) and when you're traveling and may find only limited areas where your Cocker can relieve herself.

Regression?

If your Cocker Spaniel puppy seems to be regressing in her housetraining abilities, take a step back. Reduce her space, let her void more frequently, make sure you're feeding her on a schedule, and supervise her more carefully.

If your adult Cocker is suddenly unreliable, have her examined by your veterinarian. Several diseases and conditions, such as urinary tract infections, diabetes, incontinence, canine cognitive dysfunction, and separation anxiety, can cause what appear to be accidents in the home.

Establishing a Routine

Dogs like routines, and Cockers are no different. When it comes to housetraining, feeding your Cocker at the same times each day will help her be very regular with her needs to defecate.

Housetraining takes time and patience: lots of patience—and usually a good odor and stain remover. Just remember that if your puppy or adult dog

FYI: Cocker Spaniel Development

Stage	Abilities
Neonatal (Birth to two weeks)	Cockers are born with their eyes closed, are functionally deaf (ear canals are closed), and are capable of very little movement other than wriggling around.
Transitional (Two to three weeks)	Though the puppy's eyes will continue to develop for several weeks, the eyelids open at this time. The pup's ear canals open, and within a week, the puppy is hearing very well. The Cocker puppy is also moving much better by three weeks, though she will still be quite wobbly.
Socialization (Three to twelve or thirteen weeks)	During this time period, the puppy's experiences—good and bad—with other dogs, people, and her environment make the most significant, lasting impression on her.
Adolescence (Thirteen weeks to eleven months)	The Cocker continues to grow during this time period; however, the growth will slow as she ages. She should be very near full height by ten to eleven months. Her adult teeth begin to erupt as early as three months of age, with a full set of adult teeth present by five months (this is the teething, heavy chewing stage!). By four months of age, the Cocker begins to have better bladder control and housetraining becomes much easier at this point. At seven months, male Cockers that have not been altered may begin marking their territory in the home.
Maturity (A year to two years)	Even though the Cocker may not grow in height after ten or eleven months, she will continue to develop and "fill out." She will lose that gangly puppy look, her adult coat will begin to fill in and lengthen, and—if she hasn't been altered—she will likely experience a heat cycle by the time she is a year old.

starts to make mistakes, you need to make the whole process easier for her. Let her outside more frequently, supervise her more closely, and decrease the area in which she stays when she's not being supervised. When she's back on track with her housetraining, then *gradually* increase her unsupervised space.

10 Questions on Separation Anxiety

1 **What is separation anxiety and why is it so common with Cockers?**
Separation anxiety occurs when an owner leaves his or her Cocker Spaniel alone at home. The dog's reaction is similar to a panic attack. Cocker Spaniels tend to be more prone to suffering from separation anxiety; one theory is that this is partly because of the nature of the Cocker: a very sensitive, "soft" dog that is not particularly bold or exceptionally self-confident, and that attaches herself deeply to her owner. These characteristics seem to make the Cocker more apt to stress when separated from her special person.

2 **How do I know if my Cocker Spaniel has it?**
Typical signs of distress behaviors are panting, drooling, pacing, and vocalization (barking, whining, yelping), which increases in intensity as the owner prepares to walk out the door. Within 20 to 30 minutes after departure, the anxious dog often urinates and defecates, and can show extremely destructive behaviors (for example, digging, scratching, shredding, and biting herself). Tip: If you're unsure if your dog has separation anxiety, set up a video to record how she behaves once you've left. You might discover that the "show" is as you leave, and that once you're gone, she curls up and goes to sleep.

3 **Is there any way to prevent separation anxiety?**
You can help prevent your Cocker from becoming anxious by leaving her for short periods of time as a puppy, and gradually increasing the time you spend away. When you leave her, give your pup a yummy chew or an interactive toy (one she has to work on to get it to release a treat). Don't make a big deal out of leaving or returning. Keep things calm. And, practice giving the signals of leaving (picking up keys, turning off the TV, etc.), throughout the day without leaving.

4 **Can't I just crate my Cocker when I'm gone?** If your Cocker enjoys being in her crate and finds it to be a place of refuge, crating her may help. Dogs with serious cases of separation anxiety, however, have been known to seriously injure themselves trying to escape from their crates.

5 **Are you sure she isn't doing this on purpose? (She looks so guilty when I come home!)** Cockers with separation anxiety literally can't help themselves. She's highly distressed because she wants to be *with* you—not because she's plotting her revenge against you. If she looks guilty, she's actually responding to your subtle body language when you walk in the door.

6 **What is a "desensitization" program and how does it work?** In brief, desensitization requires you to give the signals of leaving (your usual routine of putting on a coat, picking up keys, grabbing a lunch out of the fridge, brushing your teeth, putting her in the crate or exercise pen, and so on) *without leaving*. The idea is to get your dog to no longer associate this routine with your leaving her alone. You'll reward good behaviors and ignore any signs of anxiety or stress.

7 **Why can't I leave the house?** Ideally, you won't leave the house without her for a period of several weeks, while you continue to pick up keys, put them down, put on your coat, take off your coat, and so forth. Since this isn't practical for many people, try to arrange a dog sitter or a friend to care for your Cocker during the day, or take her to a puppy day care, so that she won't be left alone during her retraining period.

8 **What role does exercise play with separation anxiety?** Vigorous exercise and play with your Cocker before leaving the house helps to tire your dog, as well as providing a period of intense one-on-one time with you. Your goal is for your Cocker to relax while you're gone, and sometimes taking the edge off of her energy can help get her to that level of calm.

9 **Are there any medications to cure separation anxiety?** No medications can cure separation anxiety; however, there are over-the-counter drugs that may help calm the Cocker, such as Dog Appeasing Pheromone (D.A.P.), and holistic remedies, such as a type of Bach Flower Remedy called Rescue Remedy. Additionally, there are now anti-anxiety medications developed specifically for use in dogs that may be helpful *while* you work on desensitizing your Cocker.

10 **Will getting another dog help?** A second dog *may* help the primary dog be more comfortable when you leave (she is no longer alone); however, both dogs could wind up with separation anxiety, or the two dogs may not bond with each other, which leaves you with the original problem—but the increased responsibility of two dogs.

Chapter Five

Living with a Cocker Spaniel

The Cocker Spaniel is a gentle, friendly dog by nature. She is recognized worldwide for her love of family and her kind, sweet disposition. The Cocker Spaniel is also noted as being a good playmate with other dogs. The only way, however, for a Cocker Spaniel to reach her full potential, is through socialization. Behind every good Cocker is an even better owner!

Cocker Spaniel Behavior

The Cocker Spaniel is a great dog for a beginner or novice owner. She is not a dog that constantly challenges an owner's leadership status, nor is she aggressive with other dogs. And this is a breed that truly wants to please her master.

With that said, however, the Cocker Spaniel has one of the largest rescue issues in the country. Cocker Spaniel rescue organizations are filled to the brim with dogs waiting for new homes. For the most part, the Cockers that enter the rescue system have not failed in their previous homes because of any faults of their own.

The main reason the Cocker fails in so many homes is that there is a sharp difference between many pet owners' *perception* of what it takes to raise a social Cocker Spaniel (i.e., no effort at all, the dog raises herself), and the reality of what it takes to properly socialize a Cocker (i.e., a daily, concerted effort for the life of the dog).

All dogs, even those Cockers born with tremendous temperaments, need to be socialized with people on a regular basis, in order to develop the confidence needed to be a friendly, social adult dog. Just as a shy dog can benefit greatly from continued efforts to make her more comfortable around different types and ages of people, a naturally congenial dog can become increasingly wary of people if she is not constantly meeting new people outside of her home.

Basically, a dog's ability to be comfortable with people can improve greatly with time and effort from the owner, or it can slide or regress, if the owner secludes the dog. Much of your Cocker Spaniel's attitude toward people is contingent on how you raise her. So, raise her right!

Cockers and Biting

Through the ages, Cocker Spaniels have garnered an unfair reputation of being "biters." She is not an aggressive dog by any means. Rather, problems may occur with biting because the Cocker is not an overly confident dog. A Cocker is far more likely to bite because she is afraid than because she is trying to be dominant or is aggressive.

With overbreeding and puppy mill activity dominating the Cocker Spaniel breed, it is not uncommon to purchase a puppy that is timid or has been raised by an unsocialized, fearful mother—who literally teaches her puppies to be afraid of everything and everybody. Timid puppies *can* be helped; it just takes a special owner who is willing to socialize the Cocker carefully.

A fearful, young puppy will rarely, if ever, bite. When a pup reaches five months or older, however, things change. At this point, the Cocker, when faced with what she perceives as a "scary" stranger, has the potential for several different fear reactions. If off-leash, she is likely to run away, to put as much space as possible between her and the stranger.

If she is on-leash (and can't escape), she may cower and hide behind you and hope the person goes away. Or, she may show a "frantic friendly" response, which may appear friendly but is really a highly stressed reaction. (This reaction is common in young puppies.) If the stranger continues to try to touch the cowering dog, the Cocker may try to growl or snarl at the person. If this fails, she may charge to force the person to back up, again with the express purpose of putting more space between her and the stranger. Finally, as a last-ditch effort to just get the person away from her, the Cocker Spaniel may bite.

As you can see, the fearful Cocker gives many, many warning signs through her body language that she is becoming increasingly uncomfortable. Fear biting can absolutely be prevented with a caring and cautious owner who works on making sure every meeting and greeting with people is a *positive* one.

Helpful Hints

Quality, Not Quantity

Many owners try very hard to socialize their Cockers and become frustrated when their dogs seem to regress rather than excel from their efforts. Often, the reason for this is that the owner is trying too hard. Yes, it would be wonderful if your Cocker could experience a hundred positive greetings with strangers in her first month; however, realistically, this could overwhelm even the most confident puppy. It's much better to have a positive greeting each day—with someone who is new to the Cocker or someone she has met positively once or twice before—than to take the puppy to a busy, noisy location just to have swarms of people try to pet her in an uncontrolled situation. Keep things quiet, calm, and pleasant and your Cocker will gain confidence with each new greeting.

If you have a timid Cocker, never push her past her comfort zone: You are putting both her and the stranger in potential danger. If your Cocker shows *any* signs of fear, or transitions from a friendly demeanor to stillness, *put more distance between her and the person* **immediately.** Then, follow the steps for socializing your Cocker with people.

Reading Your Cocker's Body Language

The key to socialization is to make every experience your Cocker Spaniel has with people a happy, positive one. This is possible with even the most timid Cocker *if you know your Cocker's body language.*

What you are looking for is friendly, relaxed body language. If you see this, your Cocker Spaniel is happy to meet the new person. If you see a transition in her body language, which is basically *the lack of relaxed, friendly body language,* then you want to stop the greeting and give your Cocker more space.

Good experiences can be built upon; bad experiences tend to last a lifetime. When socializing your Cocker, you want to avoid *bad* experiences. A bad experience is one in which your Cocker moves from the transition stage into a stressful stage, which can quickly move into a fearful or aggressive situation.

Since a Cocker may be in transition only for a few moments, it is important—particularly if you have a timid Cocker—to recognize the distinctive body language of *all* stages or comfort levels. (See "Personality Pointers" on page 70 for a complete description of a Cocker's body language.)

It is equally important to understand how to help your Cocker be comfortable in meeting new people and dogs, and how to avoid ever putting your Cocker in a position of stress. Remember, the more positive experiences she has, the more likely she is to remain a social creature throughout her lifetime.

PERSONALITY POINTERS
Cocker Spaniel Body Language

Body Language	Friendly, Relaxed	Transitioning
Head Carriage	Comfortable, relaxed head position	Head may rise or lower slightly
Eyes	Bright, happy expression; eyebrows may rise inquisitively	Loss of happy expression but not yet stressed
Ears	Relaxed against head; may also be softly pricked	May become alert and forward, or shift slightly back
Mouth	Can be comfortably closed, or slightly open and panting if the Cocker is warm or has been exercising	If panting, mouth closes; if mouth already closed, may begin panting
Body	Overall appearance is of looseness, relaxed; can be wriggling if excited and happy; may also dip into a play bow with rear end up and down on elbows if inviting a person or dog to play	Body is no longer completely relaxed; all movement may stop
Tail	Docked tails are more difficult to see the looseness in the wag; however, the Cocker should have a wriggly, lower appearance to her tail wag, with the wag increasing as she becomes more excited	Wagging slows or stops
Voice	Usually quiet; may whimper or bark if particularly happy and excited	Dog is usually silent in transition mode

Stressed	Fearful	Aggressive
Head and neck appear taut	Head lowers, giving the appearance of cringing	Head held high with rigid neck; or, may hold head lower in a threatening manner
Pupils dilate; increase in blinking; eyelids tighten, giving the eyes a narrowing expression; dog may avert eyes	With lowered head, eyes are looking upward; pupils dilated; half-moon eye (eyes move but head doesn't, exposing the whites of the eyes); tightening of eyelids; aversion to direct eye contact	Hard, direct stare; dilated pupils; narrowing or tightness around eyes
Position becomes increasingly alert, or more pinned to neck, or shifting from relaxed to stressed positions	Rotated backward and pinned against the dog's neck	Pricked, forward and tense
Rate of panting increases; lip licking; yawning (but not tired); drooling (not food triggered)	Nervous panting; lips drawn back	Mouth is closed; lips may be pulled back to expose teeth or pushed forward
Body becomes more tense appearing; Cocker may also display overly friendly body language mixed with fearfulness; may give a full body shake (as if wet); stretching; scratching (but not itchy); clawing or jumping up as if semi-panicked	Taut, possibly trembling; cringing or crouching; piloerection (raised hair along neck and back); submissive urination; may flop on back to expose belly	Cocker's body is tense and taut, and she appears to be standing on her toes; possible piloerection
Tail wagging is more sporadic; or may shift from friendly appearance to fearful to aggressive positions	Tail may be wagging but held very low or tucked hard against rear end	Tail carriage is as high as it can be and very stiff at the base; tail is usually wagging but in a very stiff manner; no body wriggle; may progress to snapping, lunging, or charging
Cocker may whimper, whine, cry, or bark	Silent, or whimpering, crying, or barking	Silent, or growling, snarling, barking

Socialization Techniques with People

If you have a friendly Cocker Spaniel puppy, finding people with whom to socialize her generally is not a problem. Most people can't resist patting a sweet Cocker puppy, and the Cocker is usually more than happy to provide lots of licks, wiggles, and snuggles.

If your Cocker is less confident, however, or even perhaps a bit timid or shy, then keeping all meetings positive with new people can be more challenging.

The following are ways to approach meeting new people and to keep the experience a good one. Even with the most confident dogs, it's good to know how to handle an unsettling situation. Usually it's not a matter of *if* she has an uneasy moment, but when. The more control you have over the situation, and the better you know how to react to different scenarios, the more likely all of your Cocker's experiences with people will be positive ones.

On-Leash

Most of your meetings with strangers will be while your Cocker Spaniel is on-leash. Leashes are helpful in making sure your Cocker Spaniel doesn't take off in search of birds or a new friend; however, leashes are actually restrictive when it comes to meeting and greeting new people—some of whom could be potentially frightening to your Cocker.

The following are some tips to making every meeting with a stranger a *good* experience.

Allow the Cocker to Make the Approach

If you read no farther in this chapter, this is perhaps the most critical piece of information you can take with you when socializing your Cocker: Always, always, always allow *her* to make the approach to the person—not the other way around. Keep the leash loose and literally follow your puppy or adult dog's lead. If she wants to meet and greet the person, and her body language is happy and relaxed, let her say hello to the stranger.

Continue to watch your Cocker's body language during the greeting for any transitional behaviors or any signs of uncertainty. Perhaps your Cocker is happy to meet someone *until* that person moves too quickly and startles her, or the person may accidentally do something that intimidates your Cocker (see "Scary Human Behaviors"). If this happens or if you feel the person is becoming overbearing and *may* intimidate your Cocker, simply move your puppy or dog farther away from the person. You can do this by calling your Cocker away from the person ("Okay, Mabel! Let's go. Time to finish our walk!"). Remain confident and calm, but give your Cocker a little more space and a break from the greeting.

If you have a timid or shy Cocker, know what her "bubble" is—the distance she needs to be from a person for her to be comfortable and relaxed. Do not allow people to move into your

CAUTION

Scary Human Behaviors

Many greeting behaviors that are natural to people are intimidating or downright frightening to dogs. If you have a timid dog that you are trying to socialize, make sure the people to whom you introduce her avoid the following actions:

- Direct eye contact
- Leaning over the dog
- Patting the dog on the head (confident dogs sometimes dislike this action too)
- Putting a face directly in the dog's face
- Kissing her on the muzzle (yes, people will do this with a cute puppy or even adult dog)
- Hugging. Dogs do not hug each other; they tolerate hugs from those they love. Hugging from strangers can be terrifying.
- Loud or deep voices
- Erratic body movements (such as a running toddler, or a person with an awkward gait)

Cocker's comfort zone; only your Cocker should decide if she wants to close the gap. If you have troubles keeping people away from your Cocker, simply say, "I'm sorry! She's in training," and leave it at that. Owners of timid dogs need to be their dogs' advocate. She will only gain more confidence through positive experiences, and this includes seeing people at a distance and remaining calm and relaxed.

Control Contact with Your Cocker

The second rule in socialization is that *you* control the contact with your Cocker. Remember, sweet spaniels can be quickly overwhelmed by the clamoring of many children, or a person who is too brusque in his greeting.

The following are several things you can do to control the situation and make the meeting more favorable for your Cocker.

- Give the person a treat to hold out to your Cocker. This ensures that your Cocker makes the approach. It also prevents the stranger from trying to pet the Cocker, reach for her, or bend over her, all actions that can be intimidating to a less-confident dog.
- Ask the person to extend his or her hand with the palm up. Rather than pat the dog on the top of the head, ask the person to scratch the dog under the chin. ("She *loves* to be scratched under the chin" usually works well.)
- Screen strangers. If you know your Cocker finds certain people unnerving, don't force her to meet these people. Allow her to observe from a comfortable distance (her "bubble") and work to decrease this distance gradually.
- Individual greetings are best. Children tend to want to rush in and pet a soft puppy (or beautiful adult) in a mob. Ask children to sit quietly and tell them the rules: no picking up the puppy, scratch her gently under the chin, hold out this treat for her, and so on. Then, and only then, allow your Cocker to greet each child, one at a time.

Breed Truths

Aggressive Cockers?

It is not within the Cocker Spaniel's natural temperament to be aggressive or dominant toward people. If your Cocker is showing aggressive body language and behaviors toward people, seek professional, experienced help *immediately.* Do not try to self-diagnose your Cocker's problems by reading books, guides or articles, or watching training videos. This literature may be helpful in explaining what you are seeing; however, true aggression needs a professional to determine firsthand what is happening. An experienced trainer can observe your dog's body language and quickly determine what your dog's triggers are, or why she is reacting the way she is to certain people. With this knowledge, the trainer can then work hands-on with you and your dog to develop a treatment and training plan to correct or better control your dog's issues.

Reward Good Behavior

The third rule of socialization is to reinforce good behaviors. This is done quite easily when socializing with people; often the attention given the Cocker by the stranger is a reward in itself.

If your Cocker is more timid and isn't at the point where she's craving attention from everyone that passes by her, you'll need to reward the good behaviors she is capable of providing at the moment. For some Cockers this might be remaining comfortable while people pass at a distance. For another Cocker, this might be touching her nose to a person's fingertips.

You can reward good behaviors with soft, verbal praise ("Gooood girl!") or gentle strokes. You can also reward her with treats. For those Cockers who are working toward being more comfortable approaching people, clicker training can be very beneficial to mark even smaller improvements, such as showing comfortable behaviors a little closer to a stranger. (For more information on clicker training, see Chapter 7: "Training and Activities.")

Don't Hesitate to Back Away

If your Cocker Spaniel is greeting someone and you notice that she is showing transition behaviors or increased levels of stress, back out of the situation immediately. Move to your Cocker's safe "bubble" distance. At this distance, wait until you've gotten three seconds of good, calm behavior, and then reward her.

If your Cocker wants to approach the person again, you can follow her lead. Sometimes the period of uncertainty is temporary; it just takes a few moments for the Cocker to determine that the person is friendly. If, however, your Cocker does not want to reapproach the person, that's okay. Say thank you to the person and continue on with your walk.

Off-Leash

Allowing your Cocker to meet people while off-leash allows the puppy or dog to make her own approach.

When in the home, keep treats by the front door. When you answer the door to welcome a friend, have the person take a few treats. When your Cocker approaches the new person, have the guest reward the Cocker with a treat.

If your Cocker is timid or uncertain of visitors, try this approach. Rather than have the person meet your dog at the front door (where there's a lot of commotion and the whole issue of someone crossing into the dog's territory), contain the dog (in a crate or exercise pen) while you let your friend in the door. Have the person grab some treats from the jar at the front door, come in, and sit down. Before you let your Cocker out of her containment area, instruct your guest to ignore the dog completely.

When you let your Cocker out, allow her to approach and sniff your guest without the person making any attempts to pet her. Don't make a big deal about your dog's movements either. As the Cocker approaches the guest, or when she touches the person's fingertips, the guest can drop a treat. If you are clicker training, you can click when the Cocker touches your guest's fingertips. As your Cocker warms up, you can allow more contact with the guest as the Cocker invites attention.

Make sure the guest knows the "Scary Human Behaviors" list (see page 73), and avoids these behaviors until the Cocker is very comfortable and relaxed with the stranger.

CHECKLIST

Socialization with People, Places, and Things

The best socialization program is one that is tailored to accustom your Cocker Spaniel to your personal lifestyle. Photocopy this list and circle the people, places, and things that are important for your Cocker Spaniel to be comfortable with in order to be relaxed in your home and in the places and with the people you visit. (The italicized items are non-negotiable; you must socialize your Cocker with these people, or go to these places!) Each week, check off what you've worked on with your Cocker, and see if your Cocker continues to need positive exposures to certain people or places, and continue to work with her. Remember, ultimately it's the *quality* of the exposures, **not** the quantity.

People:
- ☐ Infants
- ☐ *Children, all ages*
- ☐ Teenagers
- ☐ Women
- ☐ *Men*
- ☐ Seniors
- ☐ *Veterinarian and staff*
- ☐ *Groomer*
- ☐ People of different ethnic backgrounds
- ☐ Other _____

People Wearing the Following:
- ☐ Hats/ball caps
- ☐ Sunglasses
- ☐ Winter/puffy coats
- ☐ Uniforms (i.e., UPS, FedEx, military, police, etc.)
- ☐ Gloves
- ☐ Fur or faux fur–trimmed coats
- ☐ Work boots
- ☐ Other _____

People Doing the Following:
- ☐ Using a cane, walker, wheelchair, or crutches
- ☐ Pushing a baby stroller
- ☐ Playing in a group (children)
- ☐ Jogging
- ☐ Bicycling, rollerblading, skateboarding
- ☐ Driving a golf cart
- ☐ Other _____

Places to Visit (once safely vaccinated):
- ☐ *Car rides*
- ☐ Public transportation
- ☐ Local pet-friendly parks
- ☐ Ocean (on a calm day)
- ☐ Outdoor shopping malls/strips
- ☐ Kids' soccer fields or other outdoor sporting events
- ☐ School bus stop
- ☐ Coffee shop or outdoor café
- ☐ Pet stores
- ☐ Drive-thru windows (in the car)
- ☐ *Other people's homes*
- ☐ Hotels
- ☐ Stairs (with and without carpeting)
- ☐ Elevators
- ☐ Slick floor surfaces
- ☐ Other _____

Things/Sounds at Home:
- ☐ Vacuum
- ☐ Brooms, mops, sweepers
- ☐ Pots, pans clattering
- ☐ Hair dryer
- ☐ Electric fans, ceiling fans
- ☐ Washer, dryer
- ☐ Blender
- ☐ Timers, alarms
- ☐ Radio, music
- ☐ Television
- ☐ Other _____

Good Dog Play

Cocker Spaniels are often good playing in groups of dogs because they are not typically bold or brash in their play. Cocker Spaniel "meet-up" groups are located around the country to provide safe play with like-sized and like-minded dogs.

To help a young Cocker hone her play skills, or help an adult dog develop better dog-dog body language (and enjoy playing with other dogs), here are some tips to keep dog play positive and constructive.

- **Equal size, similar play styles**—Cocker Spaniels enjoy high-speed chases, but aren't too much into rough body slamming or neck biting that other sporting breeds, such as retrievers, pointers, and other spaniels, tend to enjoy. For this reason, the best play groups are often groups of Cockers and Cocker mixes.
- **Balanced play**—When a group of dogs is playing, whether it's just two dogs or multiple dogs, carefully monitor them to make sure everyone is having a good time. The body language for a stressed Cocker is the same whether she's stressed with other dogs or with meeting people. If you see your Cocker is becoming stressed (or is causing the stress!), call her out of the play group.
- **Keep moving**—It's fun to stop and chat with other Cocker owners; however, to keep the dogs' play from going over the top (and someone getting offended. . .), keep moving throughout the play area to keep the dogs moving about too.
- **Watch the numbers**—Some Cockers are comfortable playing with a group of dogs; others prefer only one playmate, maybe two at most. Recognize how your Cocker plays and make sure she's comfortable.

CAUTION

Puppy Health Alert

Your Cocker Spaniel puppy will not be fully vaccinated until she is 16 weeks old. Consult with your veterinarian as to when it is safe to introduce her to other puppies. Until this time, allow her to play only with fully vaccinated, healthy adult dogs, in a disease-free backyard, and avoid dog parks and other high-traffic areas.

- **Take time-outs**—Experienced dogs that play nicely in groups will automatically take time-outs on their own. You'll see them leave the group and lie down for several minutes before bouncing back up and rejoining the play pack. If your Cocker is not taking breaks, call her out of the group and have her sit or lie beside you for several minutes.
- **Trust yourself**—You know your Cocker Spaniel and her body language better than anyone else. If you feel she's getting uncomfortable or play is about to turn ugly, call her out. It's far better to be safe than sorry.

Practice Makes Perfect

Cockers are born knowing the basics of doggie body language: play bows, happy tail wags, and head-to-tail friendly greetings are universal among dogs. Without frequent practice, however, the Cocker's dog communication skills can deteriorate to the point where her body language is so jumbled, it's confusing (or offensive) to other dogs. Cockers that play constantly with other dogs, on the other hand, tend to have very clear, appropriate body language.

When the New Cocker Spaniel Is Dog #2

If you're like many dog owners, one dog is not enough. Chances are that sometime in your life, you will have two dogs. When adding a Cocker Spaniel to a home that already has a pet, there are several ways to make the transition to a multi-pet household go smoothly.

First, remember that not all dogs become best friends. Many dogs *do* become close companions; however, your primary goal when introducing a new dog is to have a peaceful household. If the dogs do not bond deeply, but seem to tolerate each other, you've done well.

Second, how you introduce the new Cocker to the resident dog *does* matter. Despite those who advocate "letting the dogs work it out," it is far better to make slow introductions and keep everything positive. Preventing even the first inclination toward ugly behavior will go far to acclimate the two dogs with each other more quickly. With dogs, first impressions *do* count.

Keeping It Positive

The following are some ways to help your new Cocker, whether she is a puppy or a rescued adult dog, smoothly integrate herself into your home.

Increase the goodies This is for the resident dog. Take her for more walks. Feed her more meals (they should be smaller meals but it will make her think she's getting more food). Treat her with yummy bones. Play with her more frequently. Brush her. Give her a new toy or two. Basically, make it all about *her*. The purpose of this is to help the resident dog associate really, really good things with the presence of the new Cocker.

Introduce on neutral territory Rather than bringing the new Cocker into the home with the resident dog watching, take the resident dog to a park and have her meet the new Cocker *on neutral territory*. (You'll need two people for this.)

Side-by-side walking Once on neutral territory, don't let the dogs interact just yet. Take a side-by-side walk for 20 to 30 minutes. Have the person the resident dog is most bonded with walk her; have a spouse, family member, or friend walk the new Cocker. Your goal is for both dogs to ignore each other and show relaxed, comfortable body language.

Helpful Hints

If you haven't already done so, spay or neuter your dogs. Spaying prevents the hormone swings that can make for crabby dogs (for real, not a joke); neutering lowers the male dogs' testosterone levels and can prevent squabbles. Altering also prevents unwanted litters.

Keep 'em separated Even if the dogs seem to be getting along well when you've returned home, keep them separated with dog barriers or put the new dog in a crate. Watch for *any* signs of stress or intimidation (usually the new dog exhibits the former and the resident dog exhibits the latter, but not always). Prevent any outward signs of hostility by separating the dogs even farther, if necessary.

Gradually allow more interaction Continue side-by-side walking once or twice a day. If all is going well on either side of the doggie gate, you can allow a little off-leash play in a small area, such as a gated-in kitchen. Allow both dogs to drag leashes so that you can separate them quickly, if needed.

Continue to crate If you can't be there to directly supervise the two dogs, keep them crated. Even dogs that have known each other for years can sometimes find a coveted item and get into an argument—that turns into a lifelong grudge.

Be patient It may take only a week before your resident dog is bonded with the new dog; however, don't be concerned if it takes up to six weeks to fully integrate the new Cocker into your "dog" family. Jealousies do occur. Some dogs' body language is more easily interpreted (or misinterpreted) than others, and not every dog gets along well with every other dog. Give it time and keep working to keep the peace.

Communicating with Your Cocker Spaniel

Voice The domestic dog has become quite adept at interpreting what we are saying. Dogs use the tone of our voice, the volume with which we speak, and the inflection in our words to decipher our mood and our intentions toward them. As a "soft" spaniel, the Cocker is particularly sensitive to *how* you speak to her. A harsh, gruff, or even slightly stern word that would have no effect on a retriever would easily crush the Cocker. A positive tone, however, can do wonders in building a Cocker's confidence.

In addition to being highly sensitive to how you speak to her, the Cocker Spaniel may easily understand 200 words or more of your everyday vocabulary. She may be able to pick out certain words when you say them, as well as make sense of several words when strung together in a sentence.

So why are there times when your Cocker doesn't seem to understand you? It is often because she is receiving mixed signals. She may understand the words but be confused by your tone. Or she may understand the tone (that's a command!) but not understand completely what you want her to do.

It is important with the sensitive spaniel to train her with a light hand at all times, and to use your voice to build confidence, not tear it down.

Hands Dogs are visual learners. As puppies, they watch their mother. They watch what she does and how she does it. They watch her physical reaction to things they might think are scary. They learn by mimicking the actions of their mother.

As a highly visual learner, this makes the Cocker Spaniel quite adept at learning hand signals. In fact, it is quite possible that your Cocker will learn a hand signal for a command long before she associates the *word* for the command. Teaching hand signals for commands is also particularly useful for limiting confusion in a larger family. A hand signal for *down*, for example, will look the same whether the family member giving the command is a preschooler or a senior citizen. The voice command for *down*, however, can vary widely in pronunciation, volume, and intonation when given by various family members.

Facial Expressions Dogs are adept at watching each other closely for the slightest changes in ear positions, eyebrow movements, even the millimeter change that a pull of a lip might indicate. Cocker Spaniels tend to be very expressive with their own facial expressions. If you watch closely, you can see early signs of stress (tightening around the eyes, half-moon eyes), puzzlement (cocking of the head, furrowing of the brow), or extreme happiness (soft eyes, relaxed ears, happy panting).

The Cocker is not just a master at expressing her feelings and reading other dog's facial expressions; *she can read you too.* And, she will try to mimic your expressions. When a Cocker pulls back her lips to "smile," she is mimicking your smile in a friendly greeting that she thinks you'll recognize. This is not a "dog" behavior at all!

When working with your Cocker, and particularly when you're training her, watch your facial expressions. Smile when you are pleased with her; wear a confident expression when your Cocker needs assurance. She will understand!

Body Movement

Dogs have highly ritualized greeting behaviors. They literally speak with their bodies. This makes your Cocker adept at reading your body language. So, you may not realize it, but you are communicating something to your Cocker Spaniel every moment that she is watching you. Your Cocker will detect the changes in your posture, your movements, and the way you walk—and she will excel at interpreting what this all means.

When working with your Cocker, what this means to *you* is that you should forget training her if you've had a bad day. Don't try to teach her something new if your mind is somewhere else. If your body language is that of an angry person, your Cocker will take it personally.

On a positive note, however, if you show your dog physically that you are happy with her, you will see her spirits soar. Sometime, watch an obedience competition and look for the amazing, bouncing dog that does everything with enthusiasm and sheer joy. Now, look at the handler's body language. You are likely to see that same excitement and joy in the handler. It is literally contagious.

Scents

All dogs are capable of discerning minuscule scents. Cocker Spaniels, however—and their ancestors for hundreds of years—were selectively bred for their ability to scent out particular types of birds hiding in dense brush.

What is perhaps more amazing is that dogs have been trained to use this incredible scenting ability to alert patients to seizures and debilitating migraines, and alerting bipolar patients to hypomanic episodes. It is thought that with all of these instances, the dog may be picking up on a change in the person's overall scent "picture."

So, it is possible that a Cocker may have a far greater understanding of our subconscious communication than we know.

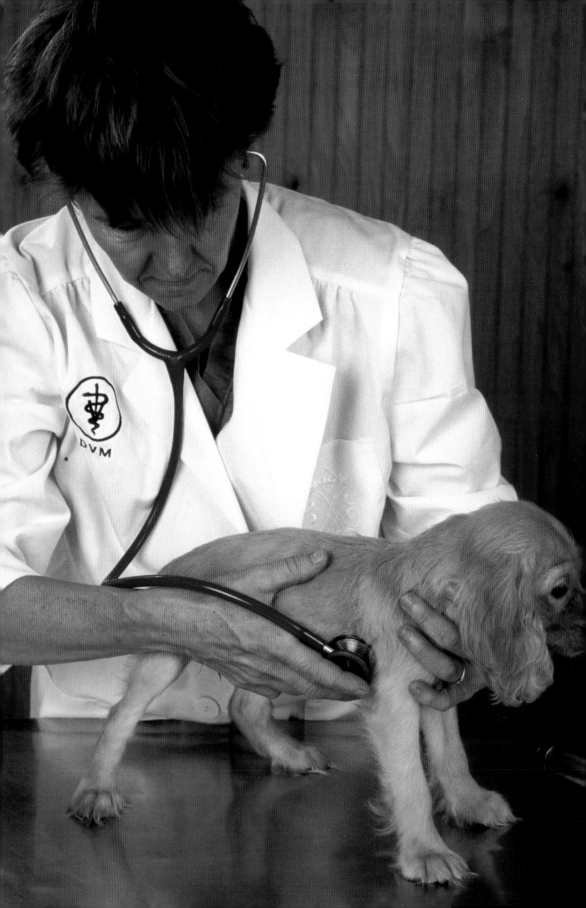

Chapter Six

Health and Nutrition

T he Cocker Spaniel is a relatively healthy dog with an average life span of 12 to 14 years. Owners can do much to help extend the years and the quality of life for their Cockers by providing the best in preventive health care, annual veterinary exams, and high-quality nutrition.

Health Concerns

As with all breeds, the Cocker Spaniel has certain health issues that are seen more frequently than in the normal dog population. The Cocker suffers most commonly from chronic ear infections and allergic dermatitis (which produces a dull coat with excessive scaling, odor, and a greasy feel). The Cocker also has an increased incidence of several serious eye diseases (i.e., diseases of the cornea, progressive retinal atrophy, cataracts, etc.), hypothyroidism, patellar luxation, hip dysplasia, and epilepsy, among others.

Cancers that are more common in Cockers than other breeds include lymphoma, mammary tumors, and melanoma (skin cancer). And last but not least, the Cocker has a greater propensity to become obese than most other breeds—and along with obesity comes an increased risk for a whole host of joint and health issues.

The good news is that many lines of Cocker Spaniels are quite healthy and live long lives. But again, the key to finding a healthy Cocker is to choose your breeder wisely. If a breeder tells you that he or she doesn't have any health problems in his or her lines, don't walk away . . . Run! *Every* line of dogs has health issues; you want to find breeders who are open and upfront about what health problems they have had, what tests they do to determine what dogs are carrying which diseases, and how they have adjusted their breeding program to try to eliminate these issues.

Preventive Health Care

Though you may feel you live in a relatively safe area of the country, no Cocker puppy is immune or safe from disease. Fortunately, the most

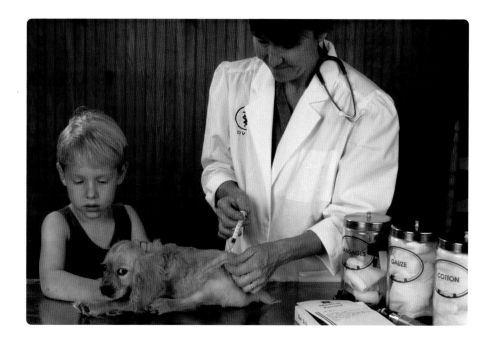

common, lethal canine viruses are largely preventable through vaccinations, and worms, fleas, and ticks (and the diseases they can cause) can be prevented with a variety of safe methods.

Vaccines

Before the invention of vaccines, the only way to be immune to a disease was to catch it. If a Cocker survived the bout of illness, her immune system made antibodies, or B-cells, that retained a memory of the disease. If she were ever exposed again, her antibodies would launch a rapid response to fight off the disease before it had a chance of affecting her again.

Vaccines produce the same response in a dog without causing the Cocker to be ill. A vaccine is much safer than exposure to the actual disease because either the "live" virus in the vaccine has been altered so that it cannot cause the full-blown disease, or a deactivated or "killed" virus is used in the vaccine that cannot reproduce at all. Vaccines with live but weakened or altered viruses can create a lifelong immunity; however, these vaccines are not safe for use with a dog that has a compromised immune system (for example, a dog with cancer). Vaccines made with a deactivated virus are safer for dogs with weakened immune systems; however, it may require several doses to achieve long-lasting immunity.

The Problem with Puppies . . .

If a puppy's mother is up-to-date on her vaccinations when her puppies are born and begin nursing, an interesting thing happens: She passes along her immunities to the puppies through her milk. If a puppy is vaccinated while

HOME BASICS
Vaccines Timetable

Vaccination	Six Weeks	Ten Weeks	Fourteen Weeks	Booster	Adult Revaccination
Canine Parvovirus	X	X	X	One year after completion of puppy vaccinations	Every three years or longer; however, the virus mutates regularly and dogs may require revaccination for protection against new forms of parvo
Canine Distemper	X	X	X		Every three years or longer
Canine Adenovirus-2	X	X	X		
Parainfluenza Virus	X	X	X		
Bordetella	X	X		One year after completion, or up to every six months for dogs in high-risk environments, such as those that are boarded in kennels, attend dog shows or performance events, or are regulars at busy dog parks	Every six months for high-risk dogs; annually for lower-risk dogs
Rabies			X	Usually one year after puppy vaccination	Annually or every three years, dependent on local laws
Coronavirus	This vaccine is no longer recommended.				

these antibodies are coursing through her body, the vaccine will have no effect. The puppy cannot produce her own antibodies until she loses her natural immunity that was passed to her by her mother.

The only problem is that no one knows for sure when the puppy loses her mother's immunities. But what is known is that when the puppy loses her immunities, she is not only able to produce antibodies in response to a vaccine (a good thing), *but is also vulnerable to catching the disease itself from her environment* (a very bad thing).

The reason why puppies, therefore, are given a series of vaccine doses over a period of months is in the hope of vaccinating at the earliest possible time during which the puppy is able to make her own antibodies, but has not yet been exposed to disease. Even when the puppy is successfully vaccinated at a receptive time, it can be days or even weeks before her system produces the required antibodies. For this reason, your veterinarian may be cautious about allowing your Cocker to socialize with potentially unprotected puppies or adults, or frequenting dog parks or other areas where a puppy would be at high risk for exposure to multiple diseases.

Adverse Vaccine Reactions

Just as there is not a vaccine that provides 100 percent efficacy (is effective in all dogs, all of the time), there is not a vaccine that is 100 percent safe. In fact, some experts note that if a vaccine were free of all adverse side effects, it would either produce a short duration of immunity or may not stimulate the body to produce enough immunity to be effective.

So, with vaccines comes a certain risk. With most puppies, this risk is acceptable, since this is the age group that is *most* likely to die or have lasting effects from contracting viruses, such as parvovirus or canine distemper.

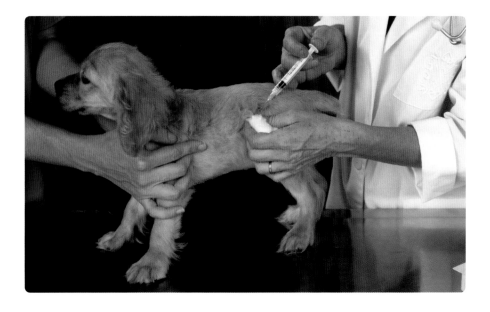

FYI: Noncore Vaccines

The following vaccines are available; however, they are advisable only if your Cocker is at high risk for these diseases, bites, and/or conditions, as most noncore vaccines have a higher rate of side effects than core vaccines.

Vaccination for:	May be advisable for:
Canine Influenza	Cockers that are housed in large groups, such as animal shelters, adoption groups, boarding kennels, veterinary clinics, etc.
Leptospirosis	Hunting Cockers or those that are in areas of the country where they could come in contact with soil or lakes, ponds, or streams that have been contaminated with infected cattle, pigs, horses, dogs, rodents, and wild animals. *This vaccine has a higher rate of serious side effects than those for core diseases.*
Rattlesnake Bites	Hunting Cockers or those that may come in contact with rattlesnakes; vaccine may limit effects of venom.
Lyme Disease	Cockers that live in highly endemic areas, such as New England. Those in other areas may be advised to use topical tick preventives as a safeguard against this tick-borne disease.
Giardia	This vaccine does not prevent infection of the parasite Giardia; however, it limits the spread in large training kennels (such as a hunting training facility). Since most Cocker owners train their own dogs, this vaccine is most likely unnecessary.
Periodontal Disease	A new vaccine to battle periodontal disease is available. Efficacy for the vaccine is still being determined. May be appropriate for Cockers with poor teeth or advanced gum disease.

However, the Cocker Spaniel is more prone to adverse vaccine reactions than other dogs. For this reason, talk to your veterinarian before your Cocker's vaccinations about the symptoms to look for, the best way to respond to these symptoms, and when a reaction is an emergency. Often, a veterinarian will ask that you remain in their offices for 30 minutes after your Cocker receives her vaccinations to ensure that she is not having an adverse reaction.

Adverse side effects from vaccinations can include slight swelling, pain and/or redness at the site of the injection, fever, lethargy, and lack of appetite. More serious side effects may include excessive pain, vomiting/diarrhea, body itching, difficulty breathing, facial and/or leg swelling, and collapse.

Another side effect of vaccinations that is rare, but that the Cocker Spaniel has an increased frequency of, is an "immunological" reaction. In particular, the Cocker seems to be more prone to immune-mediated hematological

conditions, such as autoimmune hemolytic anemia (AIHA). AIHA is a condition that causes a decrease in blood platelets, which can in turn affect the dog's liver, kidneys, and bone marrow.

The risk of an immune-mediated response to a vaccine—though elevated in the Cocker—still remains minuscule in relation to a puppy coming in contact with a deadly canine virus. Puppy vaccinations are a must. When considering boosters every three years for the adult dog, however, Cocker owners may consider serum vaccine titer testing (a test that looks at antibody levels), and give appropriate vaccine boosters only when the dog's potential immune response is below acceptable levels.

Changes in Protocol

As some diseases become eradicated (coronavirus is no longer considered a threat to puppies), their corresponding vaccines will no longer be recommended. Additionally, some core vaccines will require updating as mutations evolve, making previous vaccines ineffective. (Canine parvovirus is one such virus that mutates on a regular basis and requires new vaccines to be developed.)

And, as diseases emerge that have the potential to affect dogs at epidemic levels, you may find new vaccines being recommended. For example, the noncore vaccine for canine influenza virus was released in 2009 after the virus that was first identified in 2004.

Your veterinarian's recommendations for your Cocker may vary with the diseases most prevalent in your area, as well as the health, age, and exposure risks of your dog.

Parasites

Cocker Spaniels love to be active. Wherever you go, they want to be right there with you. If you're an outdoorsy type of person, your Cocker is going to think she's died and gone to spaniel heaven. The only problem with the great outdoors—and oftentimes your own backyard—is that the more you're outside, the more opportunities a variety of nasty parasites have for hitching a ride on your Cocker.

The following are the basics of what you need to know to prevent worms, fleas, ticks, and a few other nasty pests from infecting your Cocker.

Worms

With good veterinary care, you will be able to prevent most worms from ever taking up residence in your Cocker. Intestinal worms, such as hookworms, whipworms, tapeworms, and roundworms, are easily spread through contaminated feces or soil. In severe infestations, worms can cause anemia, a distended belly, lusterless coat, weight loss, and vomiting or diarrhea. Fecal exams can detect the presence of worms. Treatment is with worming medications. Prevention, however, is possible with broad-spectrum heartworm preventives.

Heartworms are transmitted by infected mosquitoes. Heartworm is present in all areas of the country and is considered a year-round threat. Infestations often can be fatal, as adult worms reside in the infected dog's heart and lungs. Symptoms of a heartworm infestation include a cough, followed by listlessness and weight loss. A blood sample is used to determine the presence of heartworm. Veterinary treatment is possible, but it remains costly and not without significant risks. It is much easier and safer to give your Cocker a monthly heartworm preventive. These broad-spectrum preventives also protect against many intestinal worms, too.

BE PREPARED! External Parasites

To make sure that your Cocker doesn't suffer from these external parasites, here are some preventive measures you can take.

Parasite	Detection	Removal	Prevention
Flea	Red dots (bites) the size of a pin head; flea dirt—tiny pieces of dirt that when placed on a wet paper towel appear to "bleed" (they contain blood); visual confirmation of flea in dog's coat	Flea combs (not very effective; fleas are fast); flea dips and shampoos	Monthly, topical prescription flea preventives; oral prescription preventive (6 months); some topical heartworm preventives also are effective with fleas
Tick	Tick bite; tick lodged in dog's skin or crawling	Do not twist tick, as the head may remain in the dog's skin and cause a secondary infection; pull straight out; use tick dip or shampoo	Monthly, topical prescription flea and tick preventive; some topical heartworm preventives also are effective with ticks
Mites	Patches of hair loss; itching; skin infections; skin scraping required for diagnosis	Healthy Cockers usually have no problems; provide a good diet and clean environment; work to lower dog's stress level	Veterinary treatment to control mites; treat localized infections

Fleas, Ticks, and Mange

A flea can bite four hundred times in one day, and a single female can lay two thousand eggs. Some cockers are so allergic to fleas that *one bite* can cause a serious allergic reaction. Scratching fleas can cause terrible mats in a Cocker's coat, as well as "hot spots," or areas of moist dermatitis (skin infection).

Ticks are no better. Different ticks can carry different bacterial diseases. Depending on where you live, a single tick bite may expose your Cocker to Lyme disease, canine ehrlichiosis, canine anaplasmosis, or Rocky Mountain spotted fever.

And then there's mange. Cocker Spaniels that are under stress, suffering from disease, or have been fed a poor diet seem to be more susceptible to the effects of demodotic mange (caused by the *demodes canis* mite). An infestation of this type of mite can cause terrible hair loss, starting at the dog's

muzzle and head and progressing toward her rear end. Sarcoptic mange, or scabies, is also caused by a mite—and is contagious to humans.

Pesky Protozoa

Protozoa are microscopic organisms that can wreak havoc with your Cocker Spaniel's health. There are several different types of protozoan parasites that cause explosive, watery stools. These parasites tend to be transferred through the ingestion of infected animal stools, or the ingestion of an infected animal. Giardia, however, is one protozoan that can be ingested through contaminated drinking water.

It may be difficult to prevent a hunting dog, or a Cocker that is out on a hike, from drinking from a freshwater stream, pond, river, or lake. If your Cocker takes a sip from the occasional water source, or swims regularly in fresh water, you should be on the lookout for symptoms of a protozoan infection.

Protozoan infections can become quite serious in a short amount of time. The only way to eradicate protozoa is with prescription medications, so don't delay in having your Cocker tested for shedding protozoa. Also, remember that protozoa are zoonotic; they can infect people too.

BE PREPARED! Spay/Neuter Risks and Benefits

Beyond population control, there are additional benefits—and some health risks—associated with the spay/neuter of the Cocker Spaniel.

Male	Female
+ may reduce marking indoors	+ eliminates need for doggie diapers
+ may reduce aggression toward other dogs	+ eliminates mood swings caused by fluctuations in hormones
+ eliminates the small risk of testicular cancer	+ *greatly* reduces the risk of mammary tumors, for which Cockers are at very high risk
+ reduces risk of non-cancerous prostate disorders (which occurs in more than 80 percent of intact dogs over the age of 5)	+ nearly eliminates the risk of pyometra (which affects 23 percent of intact female dogs)
+ may reduce the risk of diabetes	− causes urinary spay incontinence in 4 to 20 percent of Cockers; breed is recognized as having a higher incidence of spay incontinence than other breeds

− triples risk of hypothyroidism
− triples risk of obesity
− increases risk of progressing from mild to severe geriatric cognitive impairment
− increases risk of adverse reactions to vaccinations by 27 to 30 percent

Spay/Neuter

The only way to prevent unplanned pregnancies and unwanted matings is to spay or neuter your Cocker Spaniel. Even if you have a fenced backyard and are vigilant in making sure your Cocker never gets loose, you may not be able to control what jumps *into* your backyard.

When determining whether to alter your Cocker Spaniel, it is important to weigh the benefits and drawbacks to spaying and neutering, as well as how certain health conditions may be controlled. For example, urinary spay continence is often easily managed with an inexpensive, twice-daily medication. Hypothyroidism, should it occur, is economically managed with medication. The risk of obesity, caused by metabolism changes associated with altering, can be greatly lessened through exercise and food portion control.

So, although there are some increased risks with altering your pet, spaying or neutering your Cocker Spaniel is often the right choice for many pet owners.

Cocker Spaniel Diseases

Every breed has its own unique list of genetic diseases and conditions that it tends to be more susceptible to than other breeds. The Cocker Spaniel is no different.

The Cocker Spaniel is predisposed to many illnesses, some of which are hereditary and some of which are related to her unique conformation. Then there are some that the Cocker suffers from for no known reason; they just do.

Whether or not you've purchased a puppy from a reputable breeder (who tests for every hereditary disease possible), it pays to be aware of common Cocker health issues. The best prognosis is an early diagnosis. Your Cocker can't tell you what's wrong, but if you recognize the early symptoms of the most common diseases and conditions of the general Cocker Spaniel population, you can get your Cocker necessary veterinary help as soon as possible.

The Big Three: Eyes, Ears, and Skin

If there's going to be a health problem with Cocker Spaniels, it's usually going to be something to do with the dog's eyes, ears, or skin. Sometimes an unlucky dog will win the trifecta of poor health and have issues with all three.

The good news, if there is ever good news when it comes to canine illnesses, is that most eye, ear, and skin problems that Cockers tend to suffer from are not fatal. The bad news is that the most common Cocker disorders are either chronic, requiring lifetime management, or serious enough to require surgery.

The following list is not by any means comprehensive, but it does cover the most commonly seen disorders of the Cocker Spaniel.

Eyes

Cataracts, cherry eye, and glaucoma are eye disorders that tend to plague the Cocker Spaniel.

Cataracts Cataracts are white opacities that form in the lens of a dog's eye. Depending on size and growth rate, a cataract can impair a Cocker's vision or cause total blindness. Cockers suffer from an inherited form of cataracts; however, it is possible for a Cocker to develop cataracts from other causes, such as viral infections (for example, canine parvovirus), an injury, or a poor diet. Surgical removal of a cataract can help restore some vision to the Cocker's afflicted eye.

Cherry Eye When the gland of a dog's third eyelid prolapses, it protrudes and becomes inflamed, irritated, and red in appearance (thus the name "cherry" eye). The condition is thought to have a hereditary influence; however, it seems to be exacerbated by high levels of stress. Often the condition will go away on its own after a few weeks. If it doesn't, new surgical procedures are available that have a high rate of success in correcting the problem without causing the Cocker "dry eye" later in life.

Glaucoma Cockers have recorded one of the highest incidences of glaucoma of all dog breeds, with females more predisposed than males. This is a serious eye disease that if not treated immediately with medications and possibly surgery can result in blindness. Symptoms include cloudiness, swelling, pain (rubbing of eyes), discharge, and dilated pupils.

Other Eye Disorders

Occurring in the Cocker Spaniel, but not with quite the frequency of cataracts, cherry eye, and glaucoma, are several hereditary eye diseases. Cocker Spaniels are predisposed to the following additional diseases or conditions:

- **Progressive Retinal Atrophy** (a degeneration of the retina)
- **Keratoconjunctivitis Sicca** (Dry Eye Syndrome, causes a reduction in tear production)
- **Corneal dystrophy** (a whitening of one or more corneal layers)
- **Distichaisis** (eyelid hairs that because of their location can cause eye irritation and corneal scratches)
- **Ectropian** (droopy eyelids, predisposes to eye infections)
- **Entropian** (inversion of the eyelid causing eye irritation and corneal scratching)

Ears

Ear infections are the bane of the Cocker Spaniel. There are many possible causes for chronic infections, including allergies. It doesn't help, of course, that some Cockers' ears are exceptionally hairy, which limits proper airflow to the ear canals. Canine ear canals are different too: They are horizontal and do not drain well.

Add to all of these factors the fact that the Cocker Spaniel has long, pendulous ears, which tend to stay constantly warm and moist, and you have the potential for some horrendous ear infections.

Symptoms of an ear infection include redness; inflammation; dark, crusty discharge; blood; heat (the ear may be so swollen that it feels hot to the touch); and a sharp, offensive odor. Ear infections are painful, and the Cocker may be seen scratching her ears, shaking her head repeatedly, walking with a tilted head, rubbing her ears on the floor, whimpering, or avoiding human touch (or being reactive to touch). She may even appear to be off-balance.

Ear infections may be treated with oral and topical antibiotics, as well as steroids (to reduce inflammation). Chronic ear infections in the Cocker

Breed Truths

Ear infections can be time consuming and expensive to treat (often $200 or more per episode). If left untreated, however, the infection can have such a devastating effect on the Cocker Spaniel that it requires a total ear canal ablation (TECA). TECA is the removal of the entire ear canal. It is not uncommon for neglected Cockers, aged slightly more than a year old, to enter Cocker Spaniel rescues requiring this surgery.

Spaniel are usually caused by allergies, or a skin condition called primary seborrhea (see below). Determining and treating the cause of a Cocker's ear infections is critical to the health of your Cocker.

Keeping your Cocker's ears clean and checking them for infection on a regular basis should be part of a twice-weekly grooming ritual. For more information on proper ear care, see "Ear Maintenance," page 141.

Other Ear Issues

Deafness The Cocker Spaniel has been reported to suffer from congenital deafness. This disorder is associated with white pigmentation and blue eyes. Deafness in one or both ears occurs when the blood supply to a puppy's inner ear or cochlea degenerates, usually at three to four weeks of age.

Cockers that are deaf in one ear usually adjust quite nicely; many owners never realize their puppies or dogs have a hearing disability. A Cocker that is deaf in both ears, however, requires an experienced, patient dog owner who is willing to work with the deaf Cocker and meet the needs of this special dog.

Helpful Hints

Support for Deaf Cockers

The Deaf Dog Education Action Fund (DDEAF) is an excellent resource for owners of deaf Cocker puppies or adult dogs. DDEAF maintains a comprehensive website at *www.deafdogs.org* that provides training tips, resources, information on teaching sign language to your deaf dog, and using a vibrating collar (it takes the place of calling the dog's name).

Skin

The skin problems of a Cocker Spaniel are distinctive: greasy, scaly skin that emits a rather horrifically foul-smelling odor. This condition, seborrhea, can be caused by one (or more) of several health problems. If the cause of the seborrhea is hypothyroidism or allergies, it is called "secondary seborrhea," as the seborrhea is secondary to the primary health problem. Diagnose and treat the primary problem, and the seborrhea often resolves itself quickly.

Unfortunately, there are many Cocker Spaniels that suffer from *primary* seborrhea, which has no underlying cause. Though not fatal, primary seborrhea can be difficult to treat and manage. Basically, the Cocker is overproducing skin cells, including those that produce oil, primarily along her back, torso, and ears (which can cause ear infections, of course).

The condition cannot be cured; however, the use of retinoids, antifungals (if a yeast infection is present), and antiseborrheic shampoos and moisturizers may be indicated. Cockers suffering from seborrhea often are clipped closely so that shampooing is more effective and medications can reach the dog's skin cells and hair follicles.

Other Hereditary (or Suspected) Disorders and Diseases

The Cocker Spaniel is known to suffer from several inherited diseases, as well as other diseases in which genetics are suspected of playing a role.

The American Animal Hospital Association (AAHA) released the following list of symptoms in 2007 to help pet owners recognize the more subtle signs of pain that often appear first as behavior changes:

- Abnormal chewing habits
- Drastic weight gain or loss
- Avoidance of affection or handling
- Decreased movement and exercise
- Excessively licking or biting herself
- Uncharacteristic "accidents" in the home

Currently, none of these diseases have genetic tests to determine which Cockers are carrying the disease (without symptoms), or are free of disease, so breeders must be vigilant in tracking their lines and not breeding dogs that *have* these diseases.

- **Epilepsy**—Idiopathic epilepsy, or seizures of unknown cause, is common in the Cocker Spaniel, and usually occurs between the ages of one and three. Cockers with frequent and/or severe seizures may be prescribed drugs to help control the epilepsy.
- **Heart**—Two diseases of the heart that are seen in the Cocker (and are suspected to have a genetic basis) are dilated cardiomyopathy and sick sinus syndrome. Dilated cardiomyopathy causes the heart to become weakened and enlarged, eventually causing congestive heart failure.

In the Cocker, it can be caused by a taurine deficiency. Sick sinus syndrome involves abnormal heart rates that can cause low blood pressure, weakness, and fainting.

- **Orthopedic**—Two skeletal defects that are common to the Cocker Spaniel are hip dysplasia and patellar luxation. Hip dysplasia involves an ill-fitting ball and socket joint where the ball of the femur meets the acetabulum. Over time, the joint fractures, heals, refractures, and heals as the hip joint becomes even worse fitting and increasingly painful. Severe cases require surgery to correct; moderate cases may be manageable with exercise, weight management, NSAIDs, joint supplements, and/or pain medications. Patellar luxation is a slipped stifle or kneecap. Depending on the severity of the condition (it can happen sometimes or happen all the time), surgery may be required to give the Cocker relief and allow her to walk more normally.
- **Hypothyroidism**—The most common endocrine disorder found in the Cocker, hypothyroidism causes hair loss, recurrent skin infections, weight gain, and lethargy. Once diagnosed, hypothyroidism is often easily managed with oral thyroid hormone supplementation, which has few side effects.
- **Liver disease**—The Cocker Spaniel is prone to two types of liver disease: chronic hepatitis and portosystemic vascular anomalies (PSVA), or liver shunts. Chronic hepatitis is inflammation of the liver that over time can cause liver failure. Management of chronic hepatitis is difficult, and requires anti-inflammatory medications, as well as medication to help increase bile flow and decrease liver scarring. With PSVA, blood is diverted away from the liver, causing unfiltered blood to circulate through and poison the body.
- **von Willebrand's disease**—This blood-clotting disorder (in which a Cocker has difficulties forming clots) tends to be found in Cockers with hypothyroidism. A blood test is necessary to diagnose vWD.

Cancers

The Cocker Spaniel is not a breed with a high cancer rate; however, there are two forms of cancer that seem to appear at higher rates in the Cocker than in most other breeds.

Mammary tumors These tumors appear in the female Cocker's mammary glands. Spaying a Cocker before she has her first or second season greatly reduces her chances of developing this cancer. Early detection is critical to prevent metastasis, or spreading of the cancer.

Melanomas (oral) This aggressive type of melanoma is thought to comprise 30 to 40 percent of all malignant tumors in all breeds of dogs; however, oral melanomas occur more frequently in Cocker Spaniels. Older male dogs are at highest risk. Previously, the prognosis for a Cocker with oral melanoma was bleak; however, the development of a DNA-based melanoma vaccine in 2008, when coupled with surgery, has given hope to greatly increase survival rates.

Allergies

Though not listed in the top three health problem "areas" of Cockers, allergies are often the culprit of many a Cocker's ear and skin problems. Allergies can be of two basic types: atopic (physical contact with the allergen) or food allergies (ingestion of the allergen).

Atopic dermatitis or itchy, scratchy skin (usually ears, lip folds, and paws for Cockers) can be caused by any combination of airborne allergens. Plant pollens, mold, and dust mite residue are common causes of allergic reactions in dogs; however, it's not unheard of for Cockers to be allergic to a specific type of grass (usually the type you're growing in your yard) or an owner's favorite perfume.

Fun Facts

Inhaled allergies are quite rare in dogs. More typically, airborne allergens fall to the ground or other surfaces. The Cocker walks or lies on the area filled with allergens. The allergens are absorbed through the skin, causing an "atopic" or contact allergic reaction.

To determine what types of allergens are causing a Cocker's itchy misery, a veterinary specialist will give the Cocker a skin allergy test and/or a blood allergy test. Treatment for allergies may include allergy shots, antihistamines, essential fatty acids, and, in severe cases, prednisone.

Food allergies are the second most common type of allergy among Cockers and are considered to be the primary culprit for severe ear infections and seborrhea. If food allergies are suspected, the veterinarian will put your Cocker on an allergen-free diet for many weeks.

Once the Cocker is comfortable and not reacting to her food, you will be asked to introduce a single novel protein and a novel starch. (Since food allergies build up with exposure to a protein and/or starch over time, the protein and starch that are introduced are ones that the Cocker has never ingested before.) This process will continue until the "culprit" protein or starch is determined.

Cockers with food allergies require a bit more attention as far as what they eat and what they don't eat, and sometimes just a bite of chicken from the dinner table may be all it takes to set off ear infections and severe seborrhea.

Dog Food Decisions

The choices of dog foods are simply mind boggling. There are foods for specific breeds, age groups, and sizes. You'll find diet food, "brain" food for smarter puppies, high-protein diets for performance dogs, foods that slow the growth of large-breed puppies, and foods that encourage the growth of long coats on small dogs. Then there are foods for dogs with sensitive stomachs, foods for dogs with food allergies, and foods to slow the loss of cognitive function in aging dogs.

There are also foods that are highly processed, those that use human-grade ingredients, and those that are all-natural and/or organic. You may purchase a dry food, a semi-moist food, canned food, refrigerated food, and/or frozen foods.

If you want a particular protein source (chicken, beef, turkey, lamb, venison, duck, salmon, buffalo), you're likely to find it. Looking for a food rich in antioxidants? How about one that incorporates cranberries, red raspberries, and blueberries?

With so many choices, and fortunately, so many *good* choices available to pet owners, navigating the world of dog food can be a bit daunting. And, it's not always true that *all* expensive foods are high-quality.

To determine the best food for your Cocker Spaniel, you'll want to make sure that the food is nutritious, palatable, *and* made of high-grade ingredients.

Nutrition

The Association of American Feed Control Officials (AAFCO) provides a recommended nutrient profile for two life stages: puppies and nursing females ("growth or reproduction") and adult dogs ("adult maintenance"). For most nutrients, the amounts listed are *minimum* quantities required for good health. Some minerals and vitamins, which can be toxic at higher levels, have maximum recommended amounts listed.

When looking at foods, the label should contain a statement that the food not only meets the AAFCO's nutrient profile, but has passed a feeding trial. Translated: Not only does the food contain the necessary levels of nutrients (proven by laboratory testing), but the manufacturer has run food trials (with dogs) to ensure that the nutrients are digestible and the food is palatable.

Palatability

You can purchase the highest-quality dog food from the most reputable manufacturer, but if your Cocker Spaniel won't eat it, all that research and development that went into that bag of high-grade food doesn't help *your* dog. In general, however, most high-quality dog foods are *too* palatable, in that the problem for most Cockers is eating too much food, rather than not eating enough.

High-Grade Ingredients

When looking at a pet food label, the ingredients are listed by weight on the label. The first ingredient on the list should be a high-grade meat, such as beef, poultry, or fish. Avoid foods that list "animal by-products," as these include parts of the animal other than muscle meat, such as the heart, liver, or spleen. Protein meals, such as "chicken meal," are good, high-quality sources of protein. You might also find egg listed on the label; this is an excellent protein source.

For grains, you want a food that possesses a highly digestible choice, such as barley, brown rice, or oatmeal. Grains to avoid, and that many dogs develop food allergies to, include ground corn or wheat. Corn and wheat are not highly digestible and tend to be rough on a Cocker's digestive system.

Additionally, you may find that a food contains more unusual ingredients, such as sweet potatoes, carrots, and blueberries. Many more foods are incorporating high-quality sources of antioxidants and vitamins. Do avoid foods, however, that possess artificial coloring, flavoring, and/or chemical preservatives.

CAUTION

Supplementing

If a little of something is good, is a lot better? When it comes to canine nutrition, supplementing a high-quality dog food with vitamins, minerals, and various supplements can be dangerous. Before adding anything to your Cocker's balanced diet, *ask your veterinarian*. What you might want to add could create an imbalance in your Cocker's food, prevent another nutrient from being absorbed, or create toxicity.

Feeding the Puppy

With puppies, the key questions to ask your breeder are, What are you feeding your puppies, and how much are you feeding them? The answer to the first question should be easy for the breeder. Whatever food he or she is using, make sure you go buy a bag of the exact same food. Your Cocker will be stressed enough moving to a new home; changing foods will create an additional anxiety—diarrhea.

The second question ("How much are you feeding?") may be more difficult. Often, litters of puppies are fed out of a communal dish. Your breeder will know *about* how much your puppy is eating at each feeding, but he or she may not know exactly. If six puppies are being fed six cups of puppy food three times a day and none of it is left over, some pups may be eating a cup of food each feeding, others 1½ cups, and still others less than a full cup.

To make sure your puppy is getting as much puppy food as she needs, measure out 2 cups of dry food for her meal. Give her 30 minutes to eat her meal (without other dogs eyeing her food), pick up what is left, and measure it. Do this for at least four to five feedings to determine how much your Cocker is eating at meals. Pups will rarely overeat if the food is dry (with no canned food mixed in) and there is no competition (other pups or adult dogs).

Then there's the question of how often to feed a Cocker Spaniel puppy. Young puppies (seven to twelve weeks old) are usually fed three times a day. Once your Cocker has hit the three-month mark, she can usually be fed twice a day. This feeding routine will continue through adulthood.

Feeding the Adult

Puppies should usually be moved to adult dog foods when they've reached roughly 80 percent of their adult height, around nine months old. At this time, you can begin introducing a high-quality adult food. Make the changeover gradually, replacing a small portion of puppy food with adult food. Increase the ratio of adult food to puppy food in each feeding until you have entirely replaced the puppy food with adult food.

Once your Cocker has reached maturity, her metabolism will begin to slow down. One of the greatest problems with adult Cockers is obesity. Cocker Spaniels have a much higher risk for obesity than virtually all other dogs. There may be a genetic component to this tendency, or it could be that we humans are just complete fools for those gorgeous, pleading brown eyes.

Helpful Hints

If a Cocker turns her nose up at a meal, the best thing to do is to pick up the meal and offer her a fresh portion at the next feeding time. A healthy dog can miss several feedings without causing any long-term health problems. (Changing foods every time your Cocker turns up her nose at a portion can create a finicky eater, which will result in more missed meals and inconsistent nutrition.)

If, however, your Cocker is refusing meals because of an illness (and she can't afford to miss meals), the following are a few ways to make her food a little more appealing:

- Moisten the food with low-sodium broth
- Mix in a small portion of quality, canned food (Hint: Use the same product line as the dry food to avoid gastrointestinal distress)
- Warm the canned food portion slightly to bring out flavors and aromas
- Keep the same brand of kibble, but rotate the flavors of the wet food every few days.

Regardless of why Cockers tend to get fat, it is up to the owner to prevent this from happening in the first place. In part, this requires the owner to recognize when a dog is becoming overweight. If you gently press your Cocker's side and can feel her ribs through a light covering of fat, she's okay. If you have to press a little harder, or if you look at her from overhead and can't find her waist, your Cocker needs to trim down. If you have any doubts, ask your veterinarian. Most owners tend to think their Cockers are slimmer than they really are.

If your Cocker Spaniel is already in need of dropping a few pounds, begin by measuring her food intake. She may be eating a lot more food than you realized! Once you know how much she is eating, reduce this portion by a fourth to a third at every feeding.

Cut out snacks and table scraps. These calories add up quickly for a small to medium-sized dog (not to mention that very fatty foods can trigger acute pancreatitis). Substitute low-calorie snacks for your Cocker, such as sliced raw carrots, squash, or broccoli.

Calculate training snacks. If you use bits of garlic chicken for training sessions, make sure you figure this into your Cocker's daily food intake. You may need to reduce her dinner slightly, or if she's a "food hog" and will do anything for a bit of food, you might consider using a ½ cup of her dinner as her training treats. To keep her meal portion the same "size," substitute green beans for the missing kibble.

Consider a diet food. These foods allow a dog to eat the same quantity of food but with fewer calories. They tend to contain more bulk (they're less nutrient dense) and can cause your Cocker to defecate more.

Up your Cocker's exercise. More calories burned than consumed equals weight loss. It's the same for both Cocker and owner.

Helpful Hints

Keeping Ears Out of Bowls

Beautiful, pendulous ears tend to sop up a good percentage of your Cocker's food. To keep her ears clean, feed her in bowls that are smaller than the width of her head—so her ears fall to either side of the bowl while she eats. You can also use a "snood"—a socklike doggie garment that holds a Cocker's ears away from her face when she's eating.

If you're still having difficulties getting your Cocker to lose weight, talk to your veterinarian about weight-reduction drugs for dogs. Slentrol (dirlotapide) was approved for use in dogs in 2007 by the Food and Drug Administration. This prescription medication reduces the dog's appetite and fat absorption. It isn't without potential side effects, so weigh the benefits versus possible side effects when determining if this drug is appropriate for your Cocker.

A Word on Homemade Diets

After the widespread pet food recall in 2007, and subsequent recalls in years following, consumer interest in homemade diets skyrocketed. If you are thinking about making a home-prepared diet, consider the following:

- The diet must be written by a veterinary nutritionist. Recipes marketed as "homemade" diets can be found on the Internet and in books; however, be careful, as most of these recipes qualify as healthful snacks, not complete, balanced meals.
- Do not make deletions or substitutions in the recipe. Balancing a dog's diet is much more difficult than you might think. Every ingredient is there for a reason, and every ingredient is listed in a specific amount.
- Measure everything exactly. Don't round tablespoons or throw in extra vitamins because you think it might help. A homemade diet must be followed exactly.
- Don't cut corners to save money. The number one reason that most homemade diets fail (and a dog becomes malnourished) is that an owner decided not to purchase an ingredient that was important to the balance of the diet. Vitamins, minerals, bone meal, and various supplements *can* be expensive but they are vital to the success of the diet.

Breed Truths

Detrimental Effects of Obesity

Being even a few pounds overweight can cause your Cocker Spaniel to have significant health problems. These problems can include arthritis, diabetes, cardiorespiratory disease, urinary incontinence, reproductive disorders, mammary tumors, dermatological diseases, and anesthetic complications.

Homemade Diet Sources

If you'd like to develop a diet for your Cocker that includes her favorite foods, visit the *www.balanceit.com* website. Developed by a veterinary nutritionist, this website allows you (for a small fee) to select a favorite protein, choose a carb, and then pick from a variety of recipes using these favorite ingredients. The final recipe will include your choice of exact measurements (using human supplements available at drugstores), or the Balance IT canine supplements available on the same website.

Chapter Seven

Training and Activities

As sweet and gentle as the Cocker Spaniel is, she still requires training to develop into a well-mannered companion. Training the Cocker is far from being a chore! If you approach teaching lifelong skills to your spaniel as an opportunity to have *fun*, you will be amazed at how quickly your Cocker learns.

A Little About Training the Cocker . . .

The Cocker Spaniel is unique among the sporting dogs. She is the smallest of all the spaniels, and by some standards, she is the gentlest. Unlike many of the larger retrievers, which were traditionally kept in kennels and maintained by a nobleman's game warden, records of the Cocker Spaniel in the early 1800s indicate that she was a beloved house companion, as well as a favorite hunting partner. Sketches depict her curled up at her master's feet *in the home* after a long day of hunting in the field.

Sporting aficionados will be the first to relate that of the different types of hunting dogs—retrievers, pointers, setters, and spaniels—the spaniels are the softest in temperament. A Cocker Spaniel does not tolerate a heavy hand when it comes to training; a strong voice or, heaven forbid, a physical correction will crush the spirit of the Cocker permanently. She is also not a brash or overly confident dog. With today's positive, reward-based training, however, the Cocker Spaniel is not only a quick study, but an enthusiastic pupil too.

Even if a Cocker hasn't seen a field or sniffed a feather in her life, her long history as a bird dog means that the Cocker has energy, can be excitable, may act independently at times (part of her job was to quarter fields to find birds), and could quite possibly become distracted by the sight of a bird or take part in a critter chase.

All in all, the Cocker's genetics for hunting greatly enhance her trainability and your ability to mold her into the perfect canine companion.

107

Puppies and Adults

Cocker Spaniels of all ages can learn new tricks. Regardless of age, Cockers enjoy the mental stimulation that training provides, and above all, they treasure spending time with *you*.

There are some differences between training a puppy and an adult dog. Depending on the age of your Cocker, there are a few allowances you might need to make to keep your training efforts on track.

Attention Span

Everything is new and exciting to the puppy. As a hunting breed, the Cocker Spaniel puppy may be particularly distracted by things that move, things that make sounds, things that she can track in the grass. You may be working really well training her to *sit*, and she spots a butterfly. Her concentration is broken and she's lunging in the air. End of training session.

The adult Cocker is much more easily focused. If she's bonded closely with you, her primary focus will be you. That's not to say that she won't get distracted by sights, sounds, and smells around her, but she's less likely to.

For both puppies and adult dogs that are just learning the ropes of obedience training, it is advisable to begin training in an area with as few distractions as possible. That may be your kitchen or living room when the kids are at school, before your spouse wakes up, or after everyone has gone to bed.

Because the puppy's attention span is so short as a youngster, it is also important to keep training sessions very, very brief. A few minutes at a time is fine; just try to schedule more training sessions throughout the day.

As your Cocker matures, you can lengthen the training sessions so you can work on more skills. However, even adult Cockers work best with short sessions—no more than 10 to 15 minutes at a time. It's much better to work your dog twice a day in short sessions than in one 30-minute or hour long session. More frequent, shorter training sessions go far to keep up her enthusiasm and enjoyment.

Energy Level

Cocker Spaniel puppies seem to have two speeds: fast and asleep. How can you possibly train a pup when she's either highly excitable and dashing uncontrollably through the house and yard, or zonked out in complete slumber on her bed? Timing is key to training a puppy. Let her work some of her zoomies out, but before she crashes into a deep slumber, take a little time to work on a few commands.

As the Cocker puppy matures (sometimes it may seem to take forever . . .), she will still have a high energy level but will gain more focus. It is important, however, to allow your Cocker to let off a little steam before you have a training session. You can train with a high-energy dog, but if you take the edge off, it is easier for her to focus on what you are trying to teach her.

All Cockers mature at different rates. Some may be fairly settled and focused at the age of two, whereas many others may not hit this point until they are four years old. It is most important when training Cockers to have patience and not push them too hard in their training. Maturity *will* come! You may just have to wait a little longer for it.

Softness

An adult Cocker Spaniel may be a little more resilient to voice corrections than a young puppy, but don't expect your adult Cocker Spaniel to automatically develop into a pillar of confidence. This is a breed that has been known for her submissive urination; she is not a brash dog by nature.

Puppies are particularly tender, so training can be tricky in that you want to lay down the rules and be firm, but you must always be kind, gentle, and *fair*. As noted previously, the sensitive Cocker excels with positive, reward-based training, which does not use harsh physical or verbal corrections. Training your dog so that she thinks training sessions are actually play sessions is one of the best ways to help a Cocker—young or old—gain self-confidence.

Helpful Hints

A negative reinforcement does not have to be a harsh word or a pop on the training collar. It can also be the *withholding* of a reward.

How Your Cocker Learns

If you've trained dogs before, or watched some of the dog training shows on television, you've probably heard of the term *operant conditioning*. Basically, operant conditioning is the conditioning

FYI: Luring, Capturing, Targeting, Free Shaping: It's All Good!

Part of a positive, reward-based training system involves getting a Cocker to provide a behavior while linking a voice command with the action. This can be done in a variety of ways.

Luring: This method uses a treat to position the dog; however, the voice command or hand signal is not linked with the desired behavior until the Cocker completes the movement. With a *sit*, for example, the command "*Sit!*" is given as the Cocker folds completely into her *sit*. (If the command is given too early, you will end up teaching her to squat when you say "*Sit.*") The Cocker then receives the treat as a reward, which reinforces the behavior of sitting when you say "*Sit!*"

Capturing: When a Cocker provides the desired behavior on her own, you can "capture" this behavior and associate a word command or hand signal with the behavior. For example, when your Cocker is running toward you, say "*Come!*" *as she runs into your arms.* Reward her with praise or a treat to further reinforce the verbal command "*Come!*" with the action of coming to you.

Targeting: With this method, the Cocker is first taught to touch her nose to a "target," usually the end of a rubber-tipped stick. This behavior is reinforced with a treat. (Every time the Cocker touches her nose to the stick, she gets a treat. After a short time period, the Cocker learns to look for the target stick and anticipates receiving treats for touching the stick.) Once the Cocker knows to touch the target stick, you can teach her to move from the couch to the floor (following the target stick) and link the command "*Off!*" with this movement.

Free Shaping: If a Cocker Spaniel is learning the *down* command but not following a lure all the way to the floor, you can reward her for making progress by using free shaping. Each time she follows the lure a little farther to the floor, you can reward her with a treat. With this method, you would not link the command "*Down!*" with the action of lying down until the Cocker actually lies completely down.

of an animal, in this case a Cocker Spaniel, to provide a specific behavior, such as a *sit*, in response to a cue, possibly a hand signal or the verbal command "*Sit!*"

With operant conditioning, either positive or negative reinforcements can be used to train dogs. A dog will learn to provide a behavior in order to receive a reward. A dog will also learn to provide a behavior in order to avoid a punishment.

When training sensitive dogs, such as the Cocker Spaniel, teaching a command using positive, reward-based training is much more likely to result in a puppy or dog that is eager to learn more. It's a fun way to train, both for you and your Cocker.

The Timing of "Behavior, Command, Mark, Reward, Release"

When teaching a Cocker a new skill, it is important to know when to give the command, how to let the Cocker know she did the right thing, when to reward her (and what to reward her with!), and how to release her from the behavior you've just asked her to perform.

Breaking it down, the system goes like this:

1. BEHAVIOR—Using a lure or a target stick (or capturing the action), shape the desired behavior.
2. COMMAND—As the Cocker provides the behavior, link the voice command (or hand signal) with the action.
3. MARK—Pinpoint the moment the Cocker gives you the correct behavior with a verbal marker ("Yes!") or a mechanical signal (a click from a clicker). In the beginning stages, when the COMMAND comes virtually at the same time as the MARK, it may seem a little redundant; however, when you are saying the COMMAND first, and then the Cocker provides the behavior, the MARK helps the dog to understand exactly what she's done correctly. It also is linked to a reward; when she hears the MARK, your Cocker will know a treat or other reward is coming.
4. REWARD—Correct behavior is reinforced with a reward. This can be a treat, verbal praise, physical praise (pats and rubs), a quick game of tug with the leash, or whatever reward motivates your Cocker.
5. RELEASE—Use a specific word, such as "Okay!" to release your dog from her position, and to let her know it's reward time.

Helpful Hints

What is clicker training?

The clicker is a way to accurately pinpoint or mark a desired behavior. First, the dog must associate the <click> with a reward. Do this by having a supply of yummy treats and a hungry Cocker, and then <click>, treat, <click>, treat, <click>, treat. The Cocker will rapidly pick up the connection between the <click> and the treat.

Once you've established this, you can use the clicker to shape behaviors. The clicker can be used to mark a correct behavior, and it can be used to mark an improving behavior. For example, if a timid puppy sniffs a person's hand, a <click> can be used to tell her she did a good job. The clicker can also be used to mark correct behaviors when the dog is at a distance.

For more information on clicker training, see "Resources," page 167, for training websites and helpful training books.

6. REPEAT—Practice builds confidence. As your Cocker understands what you are asking her to do, and as she links the voice command or hand signal with the desired behavior, you'll notice she responds quickly to your commands. Before you make the exercise more difficult, your Cocker should be performing the desired behavior eight out of ten times correctly.

The Basics

The four basic commands of *sit, stay, down,* and *come* are often all that are needed for most energetic Cocker Spaniel puppies to transform into terrific canine companions. These commands are also essential to helping a newly rescued adult Cocker Spaniel adjust to her new home and family life.

Ready to get started? Just remember, whether you're working with a puppy or an adult dog, keep it fun.

Sit

Use a *sit* command when answering the front door to keep excited Cocker Spaniels from jumping up in a friendly (but annoying) greeting. Teach your puppy or rescued adult dog to *sit* in order to receive her dinner (it keeps her from knocking the food bowl out of your hands). Tell your Cocker to *sit* for all her treats; this helps to establish leadership in a gentle, nonconfrontational way.

To teach the *sit,* follow these steps.

1. BEHAVIOR—With your Cocker facing you, gently hold her collar in your right hand. With a treat in your left hand, slowly pass the treat from the Cocker's nose to just behind the top of her head, between her ears. This movement, if performed slowly and close to the Cocker's head, should result in her folding into a *sit.*
2. COMMAND—As your Cocker sits, say "*Sit!*"
3. MARK—<Click>, or say "Yes!"
4. REWARD—Give your Cocker the treat you used to lure her into position, and praise her verbally.
5. RELEASE—Say "Okay" and praise her physically as a signal that she is finished with the exercise.
6. REPEAT—Continue to repeat steps one through five until your Cocker Spaniel follows the treat easily and moves into position quickly. These repetitions can be broken up throughout the day. Don't overwork your Cocker. Remember, it has to be fun!

When your Cocker Spaniel is at the point where she's moving into her *sit* confidently (quickly and with no hesitation), you can begin "backing up" the command. Say "*Sit!*" when your Cocker Spaniel is folding into a *sit* but has a few inches to go before she has completed the behavior. Make sure that when you back up a command, you are 99.9 percent sure that your

Cocker actually *will* complete the behavior correctly. You want to set her up so that she virtually can't fail.

Continue practicing the *sit* and continue backing up the command, until you are able to say "*Sit!*" without using the treat to lure your puppy or dog into a *sit*. Hooray! Your Cocker *knows* the *sit* command.

Now you can practice it in other places and with more distractions—*but remember*, if you add a degree of difficulty to an exercise, you must make the exercise easier for your Cocker to complete. So, for example, if you move your Cocker to the backyard to practice the *sit* command, go back to luring her into the *sit* with a treat. You may have to do this only a few times before she "gets it"; however, the added distractions of being outside make it too hard to just pick the exercise up where you left off when you were working in the quiet interior of your home.

Stay

The *stay* command can be linked with a *sit*, *down*, or *stand* command. A *sit-stay* can be used to keep a Cocker from bolting when you open the front door, or a *sit-stay* can be helpful when you are trying to clip a leash on a very excited dog. A *down-stay* can be used to quiet a Cocker during meals (your meals) or to help establish gentle leadership. A s*tand-stay* is required in competitive obedience at the Novice level, though this command can also be helpful during veterinary exams and grooming sessions.

The principles for teaching the *stay* command are the same, regardless of the position you're asking your Cocker to stay in. Since your Cocker already knows a *sit*, the following example illustrates how to teach the *sit-stay*.

1. Snap a leash to your Cocker's collar. Since you will be moving back and forth to your Cocker, the leash will be important to help steady your dog.
2. Stand with your Cocker on your left side.
3. Give her the *sit* command.
4. Sweep your left hand from right to left, fingers down and palm facing your Cocker, a few inches in front of your Cocker's nose. Your hand should start 5 or 6 inches (12.5–15 cm) to the right of your Cocker's head and stop directly in front of your Cocker's nose. Say *"Stay!"*
5. Stand still. Wait three seconds. MARK—REWARD—RELEASE—REPEAT. Your Cocker should be comfortable with sitting still for these three seconds for several repetitions before making the exercise harder.
6. Add distance. Make the *sit-stay* more difficult by stepping away from your Cocker. Repeat steps one through four and then take one step to the right with your right foot. Do not move your left foot; just shift your weight to the right foot, hold three seconds, and return to your Cocker. MARK—REWARD—RELEASE—REPEAT.
7. Add time. When you give the *sit-stay* command and step out to your right, hold this position for up to 10 seconds, and then shift your weight back. MARK—REWARD—RELEASE—REPEAT. Build up to 20 seconds.
8. Add distance again. This time, step out on the right foot, shift the left foot over so that you are an entire step away from your Cocker, hold this position for only three seconds, and then return to your Cocker. MARK—REWARD—RELEASE—REPEAT.

Continue to add time and distance to the *sit-stay*, making sure that if you increase the distance, you make the time shorter, so the Cocker is less likely to fail. Gradually build the time back up. You'll want to be able to put your Cocker in a *sit-stay*, and have her stay while you walk to the end of the leash, stand for a minute, go back to her, and walk completely around her and back to your original position.

Down

The *down* command comes in handy in many, many instances. It's very difficult for a dog to bark when she is in a *down*. If you need your Cocker to be quiet, whether in the home or out on a walk, put her in a *down*. The *down* is

also a submissive position, so giving your Cocker this command a few times a week helps to reinforce your leadership in a gentle way.

Teaching the *down*.

1. BEHAVIOR—Put your Cocker in a *sit*. Gently holding her collar in your right hand, take your left hand and move a treat from her nose slowly down to the floor.
2. MARK—<Click>, or say "Yes!" when your Cocker makes progress toward the floor. (It often takes several attempts to get a puppy or adult dog to lie down completely.)
3. REWARD—Each time you lure your Cocker downward, reward her with the treat if she makes it a little closer to the floor.
4. REPEAT—Repeat steps one through three until you have successfully lured your Cocker into a *down*.
5. COMMAND—Say the command *"Down!"* when your Cocker finally lies down.
6. MARK—REWARD—RELEASE—REPEAT.

As your Cocker links the *down* command with the action of lying down, you can begin to say *"Down!"* sooner. Just be sure that when you do say *"Down!"* you are 99.9 percent sure your Cocker really is going to lie down. Remember, too, that if you see her start to lie down slowly, it's because she's unsure of herself. Build her confidence back up by going back to an easier level of the exercise. If you've stopped using a treat to lure her, use a treat again for a few repetitions. Then, once she's responding quickly again, you can continue backing up the voice command.

Come

A Cocker Spaniel that will come when called is worth her weight in gold. Sure, it's nice to be able to call her when she's out in the backyard and you want her inside. Or, when you're getting ready to head out the front door and need to find her to put her in her crate. But the real value of the *come* command is when you hope you'll never need it: when your Cocker has gotten loose or slipped her collar and is headed straight for the street. For this reason alone, it is important to work on the *come* command as much as possible, whenever possible, so it's there when you need it most.

Though you can teach the *come* command using lures, a much easier way is to "capture" the correct behavior, and assign a voice command to it. The following are several ways to do this.

1. When your Cocker Spaniel comes skittering around the corner because she's heard you gather up her food bowl, say "*Come!*" as she slides into you. Praise her!
2. Have family members grab a few treats and then scatter throughout the house. Encourage your Cocker to find you by saying, "Puppy, puppy, puppy!" (Do not say *come*.) When your Cocker finds you, and as she is rushing into your hiding place, say "*Come!*" Reward her with a handful of treats.
3. When in the backyard, make eye contact with your Cocker, smile, and then take off running away from her. Turn around. When she comes barreling into you, say "*Come!*" Reward her with lots of praise and pats.
4. When on-leash (on walks), wait until your Cocker is a little distracted and start walking backward. When she looks up, encourage her to follow you (squeak a favorite toy), and as she turns toward you, say "*Come!*"

Practice, practice, practice. Think of any excuse to get your Cocker to turn and run toward you, and link the *come* command with this action. Avoid saying the command unless you are almost completely sure that she will come when you call her. It takes only *one time* of her ignoring you or getting confused to require days or even weeks to bring her back up to the same level of reliability as she was before she didn't come when you called her.

Walking Nicely On-Leash

Depending on your Cocker Spaniel's age and her history, you will most likely have one of two possible issues with walking on-leash. If your puppy is young, she likely has no idea what a leash is other than it looks like a great chewie. If you pull, she will plant herself and pull back. It's a natural reaction.

On the other hand, if you've adopted an adult Cocker *or* maybe you didn't walk your puppy much when she was young and now she's older, you've probably got the opposite problems. Instead of having to persuade your Cocker to follow you, you've got a dog that wants to pull and take *you* for a walk.

Both problems can be easily solved.

Method 1: Persuading the young puppy to walk with you.

1. Attach a *very* lightweight leash with a small clip to your puppy's collar. She will try to chew on the leash and wrap herself up in it, but don't chastise her. Ignore this behavior.

2. **LURE**—With a treat in your left hand and the leash in the right, lure your puppy to follow a few steps with you. You can use your voice, too, saying her name or "Puppy, puppy, puppy!" or "Let's go!" or other words of encouragement.

3. **MARK**—<Click>, or say "Yes!" when she follows next to you on a slack leash.

4. **REWARD**—Give her the treat.

5. Continue luring, marking, and rewarding your puppy for walking nicely next to you.

Young puppies usually don't have the endurance and strength to walk very far, but keep up with her leash training, and by the time she reaches four months of age and is capable of walking longer distances, she will be walking with you quite nicely.

Method 2: Persuading the older dog not to pull.

1. Snap a leash onto your Cocker's collar and begin your walk outside.

2. Talk to her and encourage her to stay by your side. If you'd like, you can use treats as lures.

3. **MARK**—<Click>, or say "Yes!" when she is by your side and on a slack leash.

4. **REWARD**—Give her pats, praise her, and give her treats when she is in the correct position.

5. When she surges forward, *turn around* and start walking in the opposite direction, allowing for a gentle tug on the leash. Say her name, if needed, to get her attention. (Following when your back is turned is instinctive for your Cocker.)

6. **MARK**—<Click>, or say "Yes!" as *soon* as she changes her direction and eagerly catches up to you.

7. **REWARD**—Give her pats, praise her, and feed her a treat when she is in the correct position.

Continue changing directions to keep your Cocker's attention, and reward her for keeping up. Whenever she pulls, gently reverse your direction. If she pulls to the left, begin walking to the right, and encourage her to follow. Mark and reward good behavior—and keep practicing!

CAUTION

A Word on Retractable Leashes

Retractable leashes come in a variety of lengths (from 10 to 26 feet/3–7.8 m), and styles (cords and tape varieties). These leashes are great for areas where you'd like to let your Cocker run around and explore a little. The problem with these leashes is that once your Cocker is out to the full length, there is no way to pull her back in. She must have an excellent recall, or be in an area where you're not concerned with being able to control her on a second's notice.

Top Five Troublesome Behaviors

It is true that "dogs will be dogs" if you don't teach them to be good canine companions, and live by *your* rules. The following are the most common issues Cocker owners have with their dogs, as well as ways to reshape your Cocker's behavior.

Nipping

Dogs are very oral by nature. Puppies in particular want to explore everything with their mouths. When a Cocker is teething (between three and five months), she has an urgent *need* to chew on items. This passes as her adult teeth come in; however, older Cockers can get very excitable and one thing they *do* tend to do when excited is nip.

If your Cocker puppy was able to stay with her mom and littermates for at least seven or eight weeks, she has a good foundation for "bite inhibition." She knows when a bite is too hard and the other puppies stop play. What she doesn't know is that she can't bite you, even in play, *ever*.

To teach your puppy that nipping is not appropriate, you can try one of the following:

1. React. If she nips you, say "Ow!" and turn your back to her. This works with some Cockers (much like their littermates won't play if someone bites too hard); however, other Cockers may become more determined in their efforts to get your attention, which may mean more nipping, pulling, and tugging. If this is the case, see suggestions two through four.
2. Give your Cocker appropriate chew items, such as Kongs, Nylabones, and other sturdy toys. Have a supply ready at locations where your Cocker is apt to get the most excited greeting you or guests, such as the front door. If she has a toy in her mouth, she can't nip.
3. Teach her a solid *sit*. If she can't reach fingers and hands, she can't nip them. A *sit* also helps to settle and calm her.
4. If you have children, make sure you separate them during raucous play. Your puppy is likely to chase and nip in her excitement.
5. Increase your Cocker's exercise. A tired puppy is far less likely to nip than one who is bursting with energy and is not being mentally and physically stimulated.

Barking

Cocker Spaniels are good little watchdogs and will alert you to anything unusual in and out of your home. Cockers do, however, sometimes become quite the little overachievers and bark at *everything*, including you. You can control barking in several different ways.

1. Increase your Cocker's exercise and training. Boredom is the number one reason for a Cocker to be bark-happy. Challenge her mentally (through training and interactive toys) and physically with exercise. She can't bark if she's sleeping.
2. Teach the *down*. It is very difficult for your dog to bark when she is lying down. When she's in the *down*, reward her for being quiet.
3. Teach her to bark. When she is barking, link the command *speak*. When she is quiet for more than three seconds, link the command *hush*. Practice.
4. Remove the stimulus. If your Cocker barks at people when they walk by your home, remove her access to the window by the front door.
5. Ignore her. She will only continue to bark if she is rewarded for her behavior. If she barks for tidbits when you are at the dinner table, make sure your entire family is on board and *no one* sneaks her treats. Expect the barking to increase (if a little worked before, maybe a lot will work now) before it stops.

Bolting

Open the front door and out runs the Cocker. It's every owner's nightmare because it is fraught with danger. Some ways to solve this problem include the following.

1. Up her exercise! If she's going on regular, long walks, she's far less likely to want to run out the front door.
2. Teach a solid *sit-stay* and use it at the front door, on-leash, until you are sure your Cocker will not break.
3. Limit her access to the front door. Put a dog gate in the hallway to prevent access to the front door. Continue to work on suggestions one and two.

Jumping Up

This is a tough one. Not because it's a hard behavior to break, but because jumping up is a friendly dog behavior. You don't want to squash your Cocker's joy and friendliness, but you do want her to keep all four paws on the ground when greeting new people.

1. Teach your Cocker a *sit-stay*. When she learns that she will receive treats, pats, and attention only when she is sitting, you'll be amazed at how quickly she slams into a *sit* when she wants attention!
2. Exercise her more! Yes, there is a theme going on here . . . Many undesirable behaviors disappear when the energetic Cocker receives exercise, training, and interaction.

Leash Aggression

Though it *appears* to be dog-dog aggression, growling, barking, snarling, and lunging at other dogs *while on leash* is often seen in Cockers that are afraid of other dogs or less confident by nature. If in an enclosed yard and playing off-leash, these same Cockers will play quite nicely, or may even be timid with the other dogs. Regardless of the reason for this brashness on leash, there are several ways to help teach your Cocker to walk quietly past other dogs.

Helpful Hints

Help for Heavy Pullers

If you've adopted an adult Cocker who seems to be on a "mission" every time you take her for a walk, consider using a head halter. This device restricts the ability of the Cocker to pull, without being uncomfortable or painful. Head halters can be challenging to fit correctly, as the Cocker has a short muzzle, so be sure to have someone who is experienced with head halters help you fit your Cocker. For more information on training with a head halter, see "Resources," page 167.

1. Move her. When you see another dog approaching, cross to the opposite side of the street—or however far your Cocker's "safety" bubble is (the distance at which she displays relaxed, friendly behaviors). Mark when she is showing good, calm behaviors for several seconds (<click> or "Yes!"), and reward with praise and treats.
2. Distract her. Put her through a series of quick obedience commands or tricks. Reward her for good behavior.
3. Use the *down-stay*. Move her to a comfortable distance away and put her in a *down-stay*. She can't bark, growl, or lunge if she is in this position.
4. Keep the leash slack. If you anticipate your Cocker's leash aggression, she will sense your tension and this will exacerbate the situation. Stay calm and *move her*.
5. Decrease the bubble. Gradually work to decrease the distance by which you have to pass other dogs. Mark and reward good behaviors.
6. Don't give up. Keep walking her and keep working on her leash skills. She will improve!

ACTIVITIES Activities for *Every* Cocker Spaniel

Activity	Type	Special Skills?
Agility	Competitive	This sport is particularly helpful for timid Cockers, as it builds enormous amounts of confidence in both puppies and adult dogs; arthritic dogs or dogs with joint issues can participate but may need to modify some activities and/or may not be able to compete
Flyball	Competitive	Requires a team of four handlers and dogs; ability to jump low hurdles, catch a ball, and bring the ball back
Musical Freestyle	Competitive	A little coordination (on the part of the owner); rhythm and a willingness to dance with your dog to music
Obedience	Competitive	Good for ALL Cockers whether you compete, participate to earn titles, or just have fun training
Hunt Tests and Working Dog Certificates	Noncompetitive	Pass/Fail; virtually all Cockers have *some* instinct to hunt and you may be pleasantly surprised to discover a real hunting spaniel in your pet. For more information, see Chapter 10.
Canine Good Citizen	Noncompetitive	Pass/Fail; tests dogs and handlers on basic skills that are essential to a well-behaved companion
Rally	Noncompetitive	Lots of fun for Cockers and owners; Pass/Fail; Rally allows participants to talk and encourage their dogs through a series of commands
Tracking	Noncompetitive	Pass/Fail; requires some physical fitness from owner, as terrain can be difficult at all levels of testing
Animal Assisted Therapy	Noncompetitive; service	Rock solid temperament; therapy training and certification through a national organization
Search and Rescue	Noncompetitive; service	Physically fit owner and dog; good tracking or trailing dog; can train for live searches or human remains

Contact Information

American Kennel Club (AKC)
Canine Performance Events, Inc. (CPE)
North American Dog Agility Council (NADAC)
United Kennel Club (UKC) (*www.ukcdogs.com*)
United States Dog Agility Association (USDAA)

North American Flyball Association (NAFA)

World Canine Freestyle Organization
Musical Dog Sport Association

American Kennel Club (AKC)
United Kennel Club (UKC)

American Kennel Club (AKC): Hunt Tests
American Spaniel Club (ASC): Working Dog Certificates

American Kennel Club (AKC)

American Kennel Club (AKC)
Association of Pet Dog Trainers (APDT)

American Kennel Club (AKC)

The Delta Society
Therapy Dogs International, Inc.
R.E.A.D.® (Reading Education Assistance Program)

National Association for Search and Rescue, Inc.

Leash Training

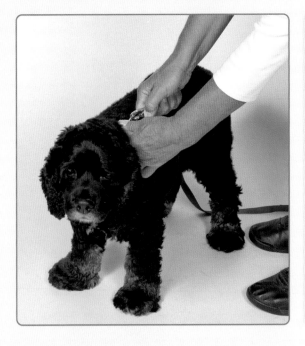

1 Clip a leash onto your Cocker's collar and begin your walk.

2 If your Cocker lags behind you (as many puppies will), do not pull her. Instead, encourage her to catch up to you by saying, "Puppy, puppy, puppy!" or offering her a little treat with your left hand.

3 If your Cocker forges ahead of you, *gently* reverse your direction (so your back is now to your dog), and encourage your dog to follow you.

4 Reward her when she catches up with you.

The *Sit* Command

1 Gently hold your Cocker's collar in one hand, as you hold a treat in the other.

2 Slowly pass the treat from the tip of your Cocker Spaniel's nose to just between her ears, which will encourage her to fold into a *sit* as she follows the treat. (Your treat hand should be nearly touching your Cocker's head as you do this.)

3 As she finishes her *sit,*
say *"Sit!"*

4 Mark the behavior
with a *"Yes!"* or if
you are using a clicker, a
<click>, and reward her
with the treat.

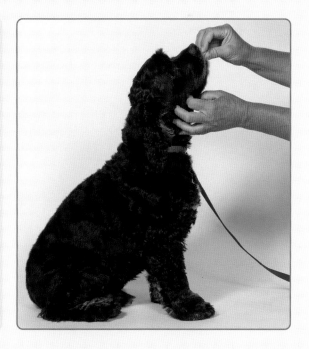

The *Stay* Command

1 With your Cocker Spaniel in a *sit*, move your left hand in a short motion (from right to left) directly in front of her nose and say *"Stay!"*

2 Take a half step to your right, keeping your left foot by your dog and simply rocking your weight to your right foot. Pause in this position for a few seconds.

3 Return to your Cocker Spaniel.

4 Mark the *stay* with a "Yes!" or a <click>, and reward her with praise and, if you'd like, a treat.

Chapter Eight

Cocker Spaniel Grooming

T he Cocker Spaniel is a beautiful dog. Keeping her in top form, however, is a bit more difficult than other breeds because of her profuse
coat. Even if you choose to use a professional groomer to maintain
your Cocker's good "locks," you'll still need to know how to do all the care
between grooming visits that is essential to the health of your Cocker.

How to Clip Nails

Ideally, you should keep your Cocker Spaniel's nails trimmed so that her
toenails do not touch the floor when standing. Front nails tend to grow
much faster than toenails on the back feet, so you may find you are not trimming all nails on the same schedule. When clipping nails, be sure to use a
sharp nail trimmer and keep at least 2 mm of nail between the end of the
quick (the nail's blood supply) and where you make the cut.

There are three things that make trimming a Cocker Spaniel's nails difficult: the Cocker's coat gets in the way, she often has black pigmented nails,
and she can wriggle and writhe around with the strength of a dog five times
her size.

Fortunately, there are solutions to all of these issues!

Furry Paws

Even if a Cocker's paws are neatly trimmed, the hair is not clipped to
expose the nails. If you're trying to clip your Cocker's nails as quickly as
possible to limit your pain and hers, the hair on the top of her paws and
on her toes will always get in the way. To help keep hair out of the way,
consider either wetting her paws (wet hair is easier to push aside and it
stays in place) or using an old dishcloth or pantyhose. With the latter
method, simply push the Cocker's nails through the loops in the fabric or
puncture holes in the fine mesh of the pantyhose. This allows the nails to
be completely exposed while keeping the paw's hair pushed back.

Where's the Quick?

With clear toenails, you can easily see where the blood supply (the quick) ends. With a dark toenail, it's not so easy. You can tackle trimming dark nails in one of a few ways. First, you can clip a clear nail, note how much you trimmed from that nail, and then trim all other nails to the same length. This usually works well; however, not all quicks grow to the exact same length in each nail. You do run the risk of "quicking" your Cocker's nails, which means you've cut into the blood supply. Not only will your Cocker be more wary of the next nail you clip (i.e., put up a *royal* struggle), but it's difficult to get quicked nails to stop bleeding. (Keep a supply of alum or styptic powder on hand to pack the end of a quicked nail. Cornstarch can help in a pinch.)

Another method is to take multiple, small cuts from the black nails and watch the freshly cut nail for signs of getting close to the quick. The mottled light and mostly dark nail tissue will begin to show signs of a gray to pink oval—that's the quick. Stop cutting!

A final way is to look at the underside of the dog's toenail. You'll see a groove that ends with an oval near the end of the toenail. That is where the end of the quick is. Every dog's nails are a little different, so to make sure you can recognize where the quick is and isn't, use the technique above (trimming little bits at a time) to learn the underneath pattern of your dog's nails.

Intense Reactions

Most Cockers dislike getting their nails trimmed, but with practice, patience, and a lot of paw handling on a regular basis, they adjust and tolerate it well. For others, toenail clipping goes far beyond just a strong dislike; some Cockers, often because of a past, painful experience, have a deathly fear of toenail clipping and will struggle ferociously and even bite if pushed past their tolerance levels. What to do if you have a struggle on your hand?

CAUTION

Don't forget to trim your Cocker's dew-claws, if she has them! If left to grow, these nails curl quickly and can grow painfully into the Cocker's leg and/or create terrible mats in that area.

First, try to avoid it. Practice handling your puppy's paws all the time. Place her up on the grooming table and get her used to this area and to the "noose" which is a small lead attached to a metal arm. Make tiny clips once a week to ensure you don't quick her, but that you're continually forcing the quick to back up its growth.

If your Cocker is an adult, use a clicker to help her overcome her fear of toenail clipping. Touch her nail with the clippers, <click> if she doesn't react, and reward her with a treat. Practice, practice, practice, but don't get into a struggle with her. If she's deathly afraid of nail clipping, take her to a groomer for her nail clips while you're working at home to desensitize her to the procedure. Often a dog will behave better for a "stranger" than her owner. If you have any doubts about how your Cocker may react, muzzle her. A fear bite hurts just as much as an aggressive bite.

All About Teeth

The Cocker Spaniel tends to have good, strong teeth and is about average when it comes to her susceptibility to dental disease. This does not mean you can be lackadaisical when it comes to her dental care, however! Soft plaque builds up and hardens into tartar, causing gingivitis (inflammation of the gums) to progress into an infection of the gums and bone around a dog's teeth.

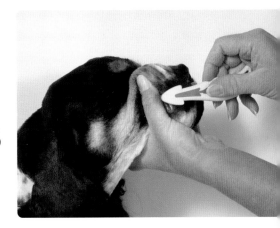

Prevention

You can keep your Cocker's teeth healthy well into her senior years with regular dental care that includes the following:

- Brushing her teeth. Brush at the dog's gum line on the outside of her teeth, top and bottom, twice a week. Use toothpaste made for dogs; human toothpastes contain fluoride, which is not meant to be swallowed.
- Provide tartar- and plaque-removing chews. Look for treats and chews that have the "accepted" seal of approval by the Veterinary Oral Health Council (VOHC).

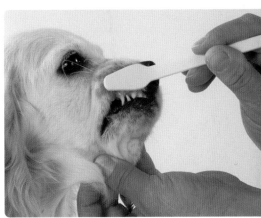

- Schedule regular, annual veterinary teeth cleanings. This is the only way to completely keep your Cocker's tartar and plaque buildup in check.
- Consider a more dental-friendly food. It was long recommended that hard kibble foods be fed to dogs to clean tartar and plaque from teeth. Hard kibbles work in cleaning a dog's teeth only *if the dog chews her food*. Many dogs will crunch a few kibbles and then swallow the rest of their dinner whole. Prescription dental foods and biscuits are made so that the dog must chew them thoroughly before swallowing and may be of increased benefit to your Cocker; otherwise, there is little difference between soft foods and hard kibble when it comes to cleaning teeth.

Brushing

The hallmark of the Cocker Spaniel is her beautiful coat; however, many owners are not quite prepared for the amount of work entailed in learning how to re-create the rather involved show clip, and in maintaining this luxurious coat between clippings.

Even if you decide to have a professional groomer keep your Cocker trimmed in one of many different pet clips, you *still* need to be able to wash, dry, and brush out your dog's coat. Depending on the Cocker's coat type (straight, wavy, or curly), and the amount of hair the Cocker has (dense to sparse), she will require brushing every two or three days to once a week.

First use a pin brush and brush in the direction of the Cocker's hair. Make sure to brush all the way down to the skin, and not just skim the surface. Mats and tangles begin deep, and the only way to find them is to brush *to the skin*.

Because the ends of the pin brush will be coming in direct contact with the Cocker's skin, choose a high-quality brush. Brushes with the little balls on the end of the bristles tangle and break hairs. The balls also fall off and leave pins with flat edges that can scratch a dog's skin. Choose a pin brush that has metal pins that have been smoothly filed into a rounded shape on the ends. A pin brush with wood "pins" is a terrific choice; however, be careful. If you drop this brush on a hard surface, the wood pins break, ruining the brush.

CAUTION

Never leave your Cocker unattended on a grooming table. She could seriously injure herself if she jumps. If she's in a grooming noose, she could strangle herself.

A slicker brush can be used to go over areas that tend to collect pine needles, leaves, twigs, and so on. The tiny metal bristles of a slicker brush will pick out the tiniest debris. Keeping your Cocker's coat free of grime will go far in preventing mats.

The Dreaded Mat

The areas of your Cocker that are most likely to "grow" mats are in the underarm area, behind her ears (depending on the length of hair in this area), on her ear flaps, underneath on her belly, on her chest, and on her legs.

Obviously, too, some textures of coats are going to be more prone to matting than others. Since Cockers can have a straight, wavy, or curly coat, with some coats harsher and some softer than others, the propensity to mat is going to vary with different types of coats.

Seeking out and destroying mats, however, is the same regardless of coat type.

Helpful Hints

If your Cocker has mats, do not allow her to get wet *and then dry* with the mats still present. This will cause the mats to "felt" and pull tighter to the Cocker's skin. Felted mats can't be broken up and must be shaved off. However, a felted mat is so close to the Cocker's skin that it is extremely difficult to clip the mat out of the coat without the dog's skin pulling up into the clippers and bleeding. Remember, it's okay to wash a dog with mats only if you are going to pick out every single mat from her coat before she dries.

1. **Spray the mat with detangling spray.** Many show dog grooming supply websites carry a variety of high-quality products that help hairs to be more elastic and less likely to break during the detangling process. These sprays also condition hair without making it oily or greasy (which would encourage it to pick up dirt).
2. **Use the broad tooth side of your combination comb.** Holding the hairs *above* the mat (and closest to your Cocker's skin), begin combing at the base of the mat, gradually picking away and working up the mat. Your goal is to break a big mat into several smaller mats.
3. **Switch to the narrow-tooth side of the comb.** Once you've broken up the mat, continue breaking it up even more with the closely spaced half or your combination comb.
4. **Finish with a slicker brush.** The slicker brush will remove any remaining bits of tangled hair that are too small for the comb to pull through.
5. **Avoid scissors and shedding blades to break up mats.** Both scissors and shedding blades have the ability to seriously cut your Cocker's skin. Additionally, cutting through a mat (to divide it into pieces, instead of using a large-toothed comb to pick and separate it) may be quicker than meticulously picking through a mat, but it causes a massive loss of hair and leaves a thin, ragged area on your Cocker.
6. **Vow to brush your Cocker more.** Really bad matting can be avoided with regular brushing. In particular, run a comb through your Cocker's trouble spots after she's been out playing in the yard or has gotten her coat wet. And don't assume that if you let your Cocker go without brushing for months that it will be simple to clip off her coat. Mats can form so closely to the skin that they cause infections. Trimming these mats from a Cocker's coat requires veterinary attention.

SHOPPING LIST

Grooming Tools

Tool	What it is	How to use it
Pin Brush	There are several types of pin brushes, but be forewarned: It pays to buy the best. Avoid brushes that have a ball on the end of the metal bristles; these fall off and the flat ends of the pins can scratch your dog's skin. Best types of pin brushes have each pin rounded; static-free brushes are more expensive but keep from shocking your dog and causing flyaway hair; wooden "pins" are terrific for everyday brushing and are gentle on the dog's skin and hair shafts.	Line-brush long leg hair (separate by parting lower hair from upper layers); brush to the skin through entire coat to remove mats, tangles, and shedding hair.
Slicker Brush	Fine, thin, short wire bristles make a "bed" of thin pins; good for brushing out tangled hairs, removing small bits of sticks, twigs, and brambles that are caught in leg and long ear hair.	Brush with the direction of the hair.
Combination Wide/Narrow-Tooth Comb	A stainless steel comb 7½ inches (19 cm) with half the comb's teeth set ¼ inch (6 mm) apart; the other half set ⅛ inch (3 mm) apart. High-quality combs are smooth and comb through hair easily.	The wide teeth of the comb are used to break mats into smaller pieces; the narrow teeth can be used to finish picking apart mats.
Scissors	Blunt nosed and very sharp.	Trimming hair between toe pads, bottom of paw, and trimming a neat leg column.
Thinning Shears*	A type of scissors that removes some hair in the coat while keeping other hairs intact.	Thinning hair in dense coats, particularly on legs and side, body coat
Cordless Clippers	These should be as quiet as possible, and blades need to be kept well oiled and sharp.	Small clippers can be used to clean hair out of the Cocker's pads; full-size dog clippers are used to clip and trim face, body, leg, and tail hair.

*advanced tool

136

Professional Groomer or Home Clipped?

The Cocker Spaniel's show clip is beautiful, but it is also very involved. It entails a skilled and practiced hand, a commercial-quality *quiet* clipper, multiple clipper attachments, and an intimate knowledge of where to clip with what blade, where to scissors to achieve the smooth lines, how to achieve the proper, domed head "look," and how to sculpt columned legs—and that's just the basics!

If you are interested in showing your Cocker puppy, or perhaps you'd like to achieve the look of a show dog, consult with an experienced show breeder of Cocker Spaniels. You will need a mentor who can help you learn how to achieve a proper show clip through "hands-on" training.

If you'd rather keep your Cocker in one of many, many possible Cocker Spaniel pet clips, you'll first need to decide which one.

Breed Needs

When brushing, always spray your Cocker first with a conditioning or detangling spray. This helps to keep your Cocker's hairs from breaking and allows for easier removal of mats.

Some trims mimic a show trim with a closely clipped face, top third of the ears, neck, and back, and a full-length coat on the sides and legs. Other trims give a more "water spaniel" (or perpetual puppy) look to the Cocker, in which the entire body is trimmed at a more moderate length. And then there are trims and clips everywhere between.

If you are interested in clipping and maintaining your Cocker yourself, the following puppy clip is a good way to get started.

Puppy's First Clip

Before beginning your puppy's first clip, make sure she is completely brushed through and free of mats. If you are clipping and unexpectedly hit a mat, the clippers can pull the mat into the blades, and along with it your pup's skin. Clipper nicks not only hurt, bleed, and possibly scar, but are a memorable experience for your puppy—in a very bad way.

Now that your puppy is completely brushed out and free of mats—and exercised (a tired puppy is much better on the grooming table)—you can begin her first trim. Remember, it doesn't have to be perfect. Her hair will grow out quickly, giving you frequent opportunities to perfect your skills. And talk to her constantly. Don't be upset if she urinates; this is submissive urination. She can't help it if she's a bit frightened—and you're going to wash her anyway after her clip. Reward her for good behavior. Give her treats, praise, and lots of love.

1. **Inside Ears**—Gently fold the ear back against her head and using a very *quiet* set of clippers (yes, they cost more but are well worth it), clip the underside of the ear leather (or ear flap), going against the lay of the hair toward the ear canal. Your puppy is likely to be very squirmy, as this is going to sound loud, so just try to get one good swipe in this area per ear. You can work on perfecting this trim each time you clip her.

2. **Outside Ears**—Now, fold the ears back over in their natural position and clip the coat on just the top third of the ears.

3. **Head**—Holding your puppy very steady (ears flat against her neck with your hand gently but firmly around her neck/jaw area), *carefully* trim *against the lay of the hair* around the puppy's eyes, the top of her head, between her eyes, and on her muzzle. She will be wiggly, so don't worry about getting too close to her eyes or being too precise anywhere. Your goal is to get her used to the sound of the clippers, the feel of the vibration, and the routine of clipping.

4. **Neck**—Before clipping, find the location of your puppy's breastbone on her chest and make a mental note of where this is. Then, feel for the front of her shoulder blades, and make a mental note of this. With her ears in your hand (to keep them out of the way, hold her head gently and clip *in the direction of the hair* from her chin down to her breastbone and out to the front of her shoulders.

5. **Neck (back)**—Now, clipping in the direction of the hair, trim the rest of her neck on the top and sides.

6. **Back**—Take the clippers and clip a straight line from the back of her neck to the base of her tail. Make one to two more clipped lines on either side of this center line.

7. **Tail**—Holding the tip of the tail, clip with the lay of the hair from the base of the tail to the tip on all sides.

8. **Under the tail**—Carefully neaten the anal area with the clippers.

9. **Feet**—Take each foot and clip hair from between the pads of the paws.

10. **Finishing up**—If your puppy will stand on the table for just a little longer, take each paw, and smooth the hair to the underside of the paw and scissor all hair that pokes out below the pads of the paws. This will give the puppy's feet a neat, rounded appearance. And, you're finished!

Breed Needs

When clipping a Cocker, or even when just brushing her, use a grooming table. These tables allow you to stand or sit while working on your Cocker, and are covered with a textured surface that keeps your Cocker from slipping. Being elevated and on a table, your Cocker is much more likely to stand still for you. To ensure she doesn't try to jump off the table, and to ensure she doesn't keep spinning around while you have both hands occupied (i.e., when you are trimming her), use a grooming noose.

Bathing and Drying

Unless you are showing your Cocker, which will necessitate an entire assortment of specialized shampoos, conditioners, gels, sprays, and powders to properly attain a swishy, flawless coat for the ring, bathing your Cocker is relatively simple. Because the Cocker does have more coat than other breeds, there are a few tips to making the process go more smoothly.

- Brush your Cocker completely. If you wet mats and then allow them to dry, you have felted mats, which are painful and require clipping to remove.
- Wet her completely. Put a nonslip pad in the bathtub and use warm (not hot or cold) water.
- Use shampoo sparingly. A little shampoo goes a long way.
- Massage, don't scrub. In clipped areas, you can scrub her. In areas where the Cocker has a long or lengthier coat, scrubbing will create a mass of tangles. In these areas, work the shampoo in with your hands from the top of her back to her paws.
- Rinse twice. Run warm water over her until you don't feel any shampoo in her coat and the water runs clear. Then, rinse her again. Pay close attention to her paws and legs, particularly if she is standing in water. Drain the water and rinse these areas thoroughly and completely again.

If shampoo is left on her legs, she will become very itchy and may wind up licking and gnawing off her coat.

- Add a conditioner. Some shampoos can dry out a coat, which attracts more dirt. Adding a conditioner will put back in the moisture and add flexibility to the hair so it doesn't break as easily.
- Rinse again—thoroughly.
- Dry with soft towels. Again, no "scrubbing" motions. Think of it more as "blotting" your Cocker dry. If she has a long coat on her body and legs, use a blow dryer on a cool setting or a dryer made expressly for dogs, and dry out her coat on a grooming table while running a brush through the hair.
- Finish with a light conditioning spray. If your Cocker is still a little damp, allow her to curl up in her crate or in a draft-free area of your house, on a pile of warm, dry blankets or towels.

Ear Maintenance

Potentially the biggest positive impact you can make on your Cocker Spaniel's health is keeping her ears clean and free of infection. To do this, you'll have to pay close attention to her ears on a daily basis.

1. Daily: Lift the flap of her ear and sniff. You'll be able to detect an odor if anything is brewing in those ears.
2. Daily: Visually examine her ear canals for excess wax, seborrhea, or discharge. If you spot anything unusual, take your Cocker to the veterinarian *immediately*.
3. Twice a week: Rinse her ear canals and clean the inner ear flaps with a cleansing/drying ear solution made expressly for dogs. Talk to your veterinarian about what product is best to use for your dog's ears.
4. Monthly: Trim the hair under her ear flaps and in her ear as closely as possible to encourage as much airflow as possible.

FYI: Home Recipe for Ear Cleaning

Ingredients:
1 bottle Isopropyl alcohol
4 Tablespoons Boric Acid Powder
16 drops Gentian Violet

Pour a small amount of alcohol out of the bottle, mix in 4 tablespoons of Boric Acid and 16 drops of Gentian Violet. Shake well before use. Using an eyedropper, put 4 to 6 drops in each ear, rub at the base of the ear and leave in. Drops can be used weekly as a preventative, after baths and swims, and more often when the weather is hot and humid.

Rear-End Cleanups

Between baths you may notice a strong odor being emitted from your Cocker Spaniel's rear end. This could have two possible causes: Fecal matter is clinging to the hair on her derriere, or she may need her anal sacs expressed.

If she has clinging fecal matter, remove as much as possible with a paper towel, or sprinkle cornstarch on it and brush it out. Then, wash her anal area with a little shampoo and rinse thoroughly. When she is dry, carefully clip the area beneath her tail and immediately around her anus. This should alleviate the problem.

If your Cocker needs her anal sacs expressed, make an appointment with your veterinarian or groomer, and have him or her show you exactly how to express them. Expressing anal sacs can be uncomfortable to painful for the Cocker, so you want to make sure to use as little force as possible. Note: The anal sacs release a foul-smelling liquid, so be sure to do this outdoors until you have the technique down.

The Eyes Have It

Cocker Spaniels have large eyes that protrude slightly, making them at greater risk for some injuries. If you wipe your Cocker's eyes with clear water and a cotton ball each morning, you will spot any changes to her eyes. One condition to be aware of is tear stains.

Tear stains themselves are unsightly, but they're not harmful. Tear stains, red or rust in color, usually start at the inner corner of a Cocker's eyes and extend down the hair under the eye and alongside the muzzle for an inch (2.5 cm) or so. The hair in this area stains this color because of the excess tears that are being emitted from the Cocker's eyes.

What you'll want to ask your veterinarian is *why* your Cocker is producing excess tears. If she's a puppy, it is very common for teething to cause her eyes to water a bit more, or, if her hair is growing a bit long around them, it could be that some hair is irritating her eyes. A quick but careful clip will solve this problem.

Other conditions that could cause excess tearing include a foreign body in the eye, an irregular eyelash, and several painful eye diseases. If a disease or injury has caused the tearing, you'll want to work with your veterinarian to solve the problem.

If your Cocker's eyes are tearing for no known reason, you can use one of several products on the market to reduce the staining effect, or continue to wipe her eyes clear with fresh water every morning.

Chapter Nine

The Senior Cocker Spaniel

I t is true that genetics play a key role in the potential for a Cocker Spaniel to live a long life. The quality of an aging Cocker's life, however, is largely dependent on the loving and diligent care she was given throughout her life and the understanding and willingness of her owner to make her last few years as comfortable as possible.

Enriching an Older Dog's Life

Do you know where your senior Cocker is? What? On the couch? Snoozing at your feet? Curled up in her bed?

Too often, just because a Cocker Spaniel slows down in her later years, her owner assumes that sleeping all day is what the Cocker does best and makes her happiest. Actually, though her metabolism may have slowed and she's not constantly shadowing you anymore (okay, she is but she moves more slowly), it doesn't mean that life on the couch *is what she wants*.

When Cockers age, they tend to get less demanding. But, rather than needing less attention, the aging Cocker Spaniel needs *more*. It is vital to her well-being to be stimulated both mentally and physically.

Getting Started

Enriching an older Cocker Spaniel's life is not difficult. Many of the enriching activities that can greatly improve the health of your Cocker physically, mentally, and emotionally are everyday things you *used* to do with your Cocker when she was young.

Exercise Motion is indeed lotion to aging joints. You won't need to take your senior Cocker out for an hour-long run; however, she will appreciate a 20-to-30-minute walk at a pace that she is able to set. The daily exercise will help increase her circulation, as well as benefit her heart and lungs. Additionally, since obesity is such a problem with aging Cockers, the added exercise will help her to maintain a healthy weight.

Teach Her New Tricks Cockers never stop learning. Take time to work on teaching her a new trick. Be cognizant of what she can do physically, and

shape a few commands or tricks around movements that she is comfortable making. Not only will training sessions stimulate the gray matter between her ears, but they will also give her valuable time with *you*.

Introduce Her to New Places, People, and Dogs If you can't get very far on a walk with your aging Cocker, put her in the car and take her somewhere she can meet people, see new things, and maybe play with a friendly dog. She might enjoy riding around in a shopping cart at the local hardware store, sitting on a comfortable pad next to you while you enjoy a morning coffee at an outdoor café, or maybe just sitting next to you on a park bench and watching the people go by. New sights, sounds, and smells will stimulate her mentally, even if she can't see, smell, or hear too well anymore.

Involve Her Some people worry that when their Cockers age, they can't or don't want to travel with them as much. For some dogs this may be true, but for most Cockers who live and breathe to be with their people, a trip with the family is a wonderful thing. If you've always taken

Fun Facts

Calculating "Dog" Years

So how old is your Cocker Spaniel? Despite popular belief, your Cocker does not age seven years for every human year. It is believed that in the first year, a Cocker is the equivalent of a 15-year-old human. At two years, she is roughly twenty-four years old. After the first two years, dogs in general "age" at a rate of four to one, or four "dog" years to every human year. Giant breeds age much faster than this rate; toy breeds age much more slowly. With an expected life span of 12 to 14 years, the estimated relative age of a Cocker would be 64 to 72 years.

her on trips with you in the past, don't think you need to kennel her when she's older. If she's able and you're willing, take her with you.

Occupy Her Mentally Every day there seems to be a new, interactive toy for dogs released on the market. If you haven't seen these toys, it's time you check them out—with your Cocker! An interactive dog toy requires the dog to solve a problem in order to be rewarded, usually with a treat. The toy may need to be chewed, rolled, pushed, or pulled to produce the treat, and most dogs are more than willing to spend great amounts of time figuring it out.

Touch Her Even though your senior Cocker may not be as active, and may not be creating as many mats in her coat that need attention, don't slack up on her grooming. Now is the time to brush her daily for the physical stimulation it gives her.

Cherish Her She has given you so many wonderful years, you know it will be hard to say goodbye. Thank her for every day she gives you, and love her like there's no tomorrow. Though you hope to have many more months and years together, when she does pass, you don't want to have any regrets.

Regular Checkups

With a minimum of four years aged for every one human year that passes, it becomes even more important for the aging Cocker to see a veterinarian annually. In fact, most veterinarians prefer to see their patients twice a year, as once changes begin, disease can set in very quickly.

Don't avoid the veterinarian because you are afraid of "bad" news. Instead, take a proactive stance. Hope for no changes in your Cocker's health, but if there are changes, the sooner the diagnosis, the better the prognosis. Many "senior" conditions and illnesses, if caught early, can be treated or managed well enough to give an aging Cocker Spaniel years more of a *high-quality*, happy life.

Whatever you do, don't ignore troubling symptoms. Cockers will mask their discomfort, so by the time you notice something is wrong, she may be very ill. At this stage in your Cocker's life, once you've discovered something is seriously wrong with your dog, waiting a few days to see if things get better before you call your veterinarian will likely make a poor situation far worse. Get it checked out when you notice it. Don't wait.

Breed Needs

Cocker Creature Comforts

Older dogs cannot regulate their body temperature as well as younger dogs. Make sure your Cocker's bed is in a draft-free location, so that she doesn't become chilled. Her bedding should be thickly padded and deep, maybe with an extra blanket on top for her to nest into.

When outside, be sure to keep her from getting chilled. She may not have needed a jacket when she was younger, but she might need one now. Sweaters made with natural fibers breathe well and are good for slightly chilly days; waterproof, insulated jackets with belly guards (to keep their undersides from getting wet and soaked) may be required for colder, wet days.

Changes You Should Look For

It is true that as the Cocker's body ages, she will experience some changes. The following are some changes that are typical of an aging Cocker and tips on what you can do to help her be more comfortable, as well as changes that merit a trip to the veterinarian's office.

Skin As a Cocker Spaniel ages, she may experience less skin circulation and oil production in her coat. This can cause her usually lustrous coat to become drier and her skin more sensitive to the touch. To help increase the blood flow to her skin and more evenly spread her natural oils through her coat, brush her. A good brush to use is a wooden pin brush. The pins slide easily through her hair, and the wooden pins are gentle, yet stimulating, to her skin.

Changes that indicate a potential health problem include flakiness, loss of hair, and greasy, scaly skin. Older Cockers may suffer from hypothyroidism (see page 99), or seborrhea. Additionally, keep an eye out for hot spots, or any other areas of irritation on her skin.

Nails Aging nails can become drier or more crumbly, so make sure that your nail clipper is sharp. If you clip a nail and leave rough edges because of the crumbling, use a nail file to smooth out the edges. A rough-edged nail could hurt your Cocker when she tries to scratch herself.

Also, when clipping nails, be aware that your Cocker may have pain in her joints from arthritis. It may be difficult for her to keep her paw in the position you usually hold it in for clipping. You may need to hold her paw lower, or have her lie down on her grooming table for nail-clipping sessions.

Teeth If you've brushed your Cocker's teeth faithfully and had regular veterinary dental cleanings, your aging Cocker's teeth should be in good shape. If you notice, however, that your Cocker's eating habits are

CAUTION

Lumps and Bumps

When feeling your Cocker, look for small lumps and bumps on her skin. Cockers are predisposed to lipomas, or "fatty tumors." These are benign tumors that can be diagnosed with a needle aspiration; however, without a diagnosis from your veterinarian, it could be easy to assume that a lump is a lipoma, when it may be a cancerous growth. Be sure to check any new lumps. Also, be aware that lipomas are removed only if they are in a location where they make the dog uncomfortable, such as on her chest (so she can't lie down comfortably) or under her arm (affecting her movement).

Warts, a result of the papillomavirus, occur at a much higher incidence with aging Cocker Spaniels. These warts are unsightly but not a health risk, and usually, if the immune system is strong, disappear within three months. Their appearance, however, may indicate a compromised immune system. Warts that don't go away on their own, or that are in the way of grooming (accidentally clipping a wart can be very painful for the dog), can be removed surgically.

BE PREPARED! Establishing What's Normal Now

When your Cocker Spaniel reaches roughly seven years of age, your veterinarian will want to run some basic tests to establish what is *normal* for your dog. Then, down the road if she becomes ill, new tests will show what is *abnormal* for your Cocker, when compared with the baseline tests.

Test	What It Is	Looking For	Indicates
Complete Blood Cell Count (CBC)	Red and white blood cell count	Abnormally high numbers of white cells; abnormally low numbers of red cells	Possible infection, disease; anemia
Blood Chemistry Profile	A test that looks for for the presence of proteins, enzymes, electrolytes, glucose, cholesterol, potassium, chloride, etc. in the blood	Abnormal levels, or those that fall above or below the normal range for the blood chemistry elements	Early indicators of disease or change in the functioning abilities of the thyroid, liver, kidney, and pancreas; health of muscles and bone
Urinalysis	A chemical analysis of urine	pH value, presence of crystals, blood, proteins, etc.	Signs of fever, dehydration, disease, and infection

changing (she's not eating very much food or is dropping a lot of food on the floor), take a closer look at her teeth, gums, and mouth tissues. A broken tooth, an infected gum, or an oral cyst could easily affect her ability to eat.

Changes in Appetite As a Cocker Spaniel ages, her sense of taste may decrease. If your Cocker isn't eating as well as she used to and your veterinarian has ruled out disease-related causes for a wane in appetite, you might try to make her food more palatable. There are several ways you can do this.

- Change her food. Find a food that is high-quality and that she finds irresistible.
- Warm the food. Heating her meal will bring out the aromas and flavors.
- Moisten her food. Many dogs like the addition of low-salt beef or chicken broth to their meals.
- Add canned food. If you are feeding her kibble, try adding some canned food to the mix.
- Hand-feed. Sometimes an older dog just needs to get some food in her stomach to get her eating again.

Changes in Stools If your Cocker is producing *more* stools than normal and you haven't changed her food, it could be that she's not metabolizing her food as efficiently. This can be an age-related problem, and if your veterinarian has ruled out other causes, consider switching to a more nutrient-dense, more easily digestible food.

Managing Incontinence

Female Cocker Spaniels that have been spayed tend to run a higher risk of incontinence. Incontinence is different from having an "accident" in that the dog does not realize she is leaking. She is usually sound asleep when she releases her urine, though in more acute cases, she may actually drip when lying down.

If you suspect urinary incontinence, your veterinarian will want to rule out other possible causes, such as urinary tract infections, diabetes, kidney disease, or hypothyroidism, all of which could cause an increase in drinking, and a more urgent need to urinate.

If other diseases have been ruled out, there are several approaches you can take to controlling incontinence, such as managing your Cocker's weight (excess weight puts

Breed Truths

Male Cockers *can* suffer from incontinence; however, it is much more unusual than in females. If your male Cocker is "leaking," have him examined by your veterinarian. His accidents may be caused by something completely different.

pressure on the bladder, which puts pressure on the urinary sphincter, resulting in leakage). Exercise also helps, not only for weight loss but to firm up muscles supporting the urinary sphincter. And, picking up water 30 minutes before bedtime and allowing your Cocker to completely void her bladder before going to sleep for the night will help.

Veterinary Intervention

If some basic living changes don't help your Cocker Spaniel control her leaking episodes, prescription medications are available. These medications are relatively inexpensive, and are considered very safe (with few, if any, side effects). They can also be used long term, and in most cases have a high to total success rate.

In rare instances in which medication doesn't significantly resolve incontinence, surgery is an option. A relatively new procedure is available, in which collagen injections are used to narrow the urinary sphincter.

Helpful Hints

Under Wraps

If your Cocker is incontinent, wrap the inner padding part of her dog bed in a large trash bag. Then, zip the regular bed covering over it. When she leaks, you can wash the outer covering and throw away the wet trash bag without damaging the inner padding of the bed. You may also consider having your Cocker wear a doggie diaper (for females) or a belly band (males) at night.

Coping with Blindness and Deafness

The Cocker Spaniel is predisposed to several different genetic eye diseases that can cause decreased vision or blindness. Older Cockers that have been free of hereditary eye diseases may still experience reduced vision in their later years because of nuclear sclerosis: a natural, age-related clouding of the eye.

Decreased hearing, on the other hand, is a natural effect of aging. If your elderly Cocker isn't responding when you call her name, it really may be that she doesn't hear you as well—and not that she's exhibiting "selective" hearing as you may have thought.

As with any possible change in your dog's physical health, if you suspect your Cocker Spaniel is experiencing either decreased vision or hearing, it is best to have her examined. If the effects are irreversible, take heart. There are many things you can do to help your Cocker navigate your home and live a high-quality life, even with vision and hearing disabilities.

Changes for the Vision Impaired

If your Cocker is losing her vision, one of the most important things to do is not rearrange the furniture. Keep the pathways from room to room to room the same. Also, don't set boxes, bags, shoes, book bags, briefcases, or other items on the floor. Your Cocker may run right into them, not realizing the pathways aren't clear.

Leave a scent trail to help your Cocker navigate the house. Usually, their scenting abilities remain stellar, and if you walk through the house each morning, your Cocker will be able to follow your track as if she had perfect vision—except that she'll be using her nose.

And finally, even if your Cocker Spaniel has been a social butterfly all her life, she may find it very frighten-

Helpful Hints

For more information on adjusting your home to make life easier for a vision-impaired Cocker, visit *www.blinddogs.com*.

ing that she's not able to visually identify people who come into your home. Ask friends who come into your home to allow your Cocker to make the approach. Also ask that they allow her to sniff their hands first and then scratch her under the chin, so as not to startle her.

Working with Hearing Impairments

The biggest issue with hearing loss in the dog occurs when the Cocker is sound asleep. When you call her name, she can't hear you. If you touch or shake her a little to wake her up, her reaction is not going to be the same as a sleepy child. A deaf Cocker who is startled out of a deep sleep (and maybe can't see too well either) may respond by snapping.

To resolve this issue, create a new "alert" signal for your Cocker. Many owners of deaf dogs use battery-operated vibrating collars for this purpose. You would train with the collar the same way you would train a dog to a clicker: <buzz>, treat, <buzz>, treat, <buzz>, treat, <buzz>, treat, etc., until the dog knows that a buzz on the collar means she's getting a treat—and she should find you. From there, you can teach her hand signals for all the commands she already knows.

Cognitive Dysfunction Syndrome (CDS)

The older a dog lives, the more likely she is to suffer from cognitive dysfunction syndrome (CDS). A study found that 28 percent of dogs aged 11 years or older had at least one sign of CDS. So, it is often with mixed emotions that Cocker Spaniel owners look at their dogs as they approach a more advanced age.

There are currently no cures for CDS. There are also no known preventives. The current goal of treatment, once all other possible diseases and conditions have been ruled out that might cause a dog to exhibit some of the symptoms of cognitive loss (such as arthritis, tooth decay, or endocrine disease), is to slow the progression of cognitive decline.

Diet A prescription diet that was developed in 2004 by Hill's Pet Nutrition (Canine b/d®) was proven to be effective in improving the performance of dogs suffering from CDS on a number of cognitive tests.

BE PREPARED! Symptoms of CDS

These are the four most common early symptoms of CDS:

Symptom	Description of Behaviors
Disorientation	A dog seems confused about how to use a dog door (after having one all her life); runs to the wrong door to be let out; may stand behind an open door and not understand why she can't walk forward.
Variances in social behaviors	A Cocker may stop joyfully greeting her owner after work, as if he or she is a stranger; sudden aggression or unexplained timidity; odd behaviors around other dogs.
Interrupted sleep cycle	Restlessness at night but heavy slumber during the day; waking up multiple times during the night but not needing to relieve herself.
Loss of housetraining	Accidents in the home that are not related to incontinence, disease, or separation anxiety.

Medications ANIPRYL (Selegiline hydrochloride, L-deprenyl) is a prescription medication that has been shown to improve behaviors (temporarily) in dogs suffering from CDS.

Arthritis

The Cocker Spaniel is neither a big dog nor a heavy dog. So, though she's not at as high a risk of suffering from painful, debilitating arthritis when she's middle-aged, she does run the risk of suffering from arthritis pain as an older senior.

Basically, arthritis occurs when the cartilage or natural cushioning in a dog's joints wears down. If a Cocker is overweight, which is not uncommon, the joint cartilage can wear down faster than in a lighter dog. An injury to a joint can cause greater wear and tear on the cartilage. And, any joint abnormality, such as hip dysplasia, will hasten the onset of arthritis.

Most Cocker Spaniel owners don't notice their dogs' arthritis until it has become quite advanced. The merry little Cocker is known for being a martyr when it comes to pain, and all an owner might notice is a slowness to rise from lying down, or a slight limp that appears after vigorous exercise. Arthritis is diagnosed with X rays, which will illustrate the position of the bones in a joint, and the thickness of any remaining cartilage.

The pain of arthritis occurs because when there's not much cushioning between bones, every step can be jarring. Movement causes inflammation, which stiffens the joint, and causes more pain. There are many ways to treat arthritis, and depending on your Cocker's age, health, and the severity of the arthritis, you may be able to select a treatment plan that provides your Cocker with good—or possibly even total—pain relief.

Joint Supplements A first line of attack for arthritic patients is a good joint supplement. Glucosamine HCL, chondroiton sulfate, and methyl sulfonyl-methane (MSM) are commonly recommended for arthritic dogs, and are given in prescription doses. It is thought that joint supplements must be taken regularly for four to six weeks before any benefits can be seen. They are believed to help reduce arthritic pain and may improve the condition of the joint itself.

Helpful Hints

Arthritis medications for dogs can be very expensive. Here's a tip: some veterinarians will offer Internet prices on medication or supplements if you print out the order (with tax and shipping) and bring the printout to the clinic.

NSAIDs Non-steroidal anti-inflammatory drugs (NSAIDs) are effective in reducing inflammation from arthritis and increasing a dog's mobility and comfort. For some arthritic dogs,

NSAIDs are like a new lease on life; after taking these medications, they bounce around like puppies. Well, more like older dogs that think they're puppies, but it's an amazing sight when the medications work for a dog. They don't work for every dog, of course, and some dogs can suffer serious side effects from taking NSAIDs.

Pain Medications If an arthritic Cocker can't take NSAIDs, or if the NSAIDs aren't giving her enough relief, any number of pain medications might be prescribed. Painkillers won't reduce inflammation; however, they can limit the dog's pain. Many medications available today do not cause drowsiness or alter your dog's temperament in any way.

Surgical Options Surgery may be a way to give your Cocker Spaniel complete and total relief from her arthritis pain. Surgery, however, may or may not be a feasible alternative for your Cocker. Factors that must be considered include:

- which joint(s) are affected;
- your Cocker's age;
- her current health;
- your physical ability to care for your Cocker during her recovery time (which could be a few days for a minimally invasive procedure to six weeks with a total hip replacement); and
- your financial capacity to pay for an operation (total joint replacement may cost more than $3,500 per joint).

All surgeries carry risks. Before signing on to have your 12-year-old Cocker's hip replaced, be sure to discuss all your options with your veterinarian and the surgeon. The benefits should always outweigh the potential risks.

HOME BASICS
What You Can Do to Ease Arthritic Pain

- Exercise—Gentle, easy exercise is best. Swimming is *ideal*.
- Maintain a healthy weight—Every pound counts when a dog has sore, achy joints.
- Supportive bedding—Orthopedic bedding, cooling gel pads, and thick, memory foam beds can provide support without putting uneven pressure on arthritic joints.
- Good footing on floors—Lay nonslip rugs and runners throughout your home or at least in all passageways that your Cocker uses. When an arthritic dog falls, it's very difficult and extremely painful to get back up.
- No slippery feet—Keep your Cocker's nails trimmed and the hair between her pads clipped short, so she doesn't slip walking across the floors.
- Elevate bowls—It can be difficult to bend down to eat when a dog has arthritis, so raise the bowls so she can eat more comfortably.
- Use ramps and steps—Allow her access to all her favorite resting places with carpeted, portable steps or a sturdy, nonslip ramp.

Are You on the Same Page?

End-of-life care can be expensive, frustrating, and heartbreaking—and not necessarily in that order. One of the greatest advantages of raising a dog in modern times is that there are amazing diagnostic tools, emerging surgical techniques, and new drugs that can treat what was formerly untreatable.

Sometimes, there's a price to pay for these options. Just ask the owner of an eight-year-old dog who spent $2,000 in diagnostics and testing, hoping to find a reason (and a treatment) for her dog's illness, only to discover that her dog had an inoperable form of cancer. Or, talk to the pet owner who was told he should have the partially torn ACL of his arthritic, deaf, and nearly blind 12-year-old dog repaired (a $3,500 operation)—and she didn't have a noticeable limp.

Where do you draw the line in care and treatments? How do you draw the line when it's your canine companion for more than a decade? You know your Cocker better than anyone else. You know her quality of life, and you know when she's comfortable and happy. What is most important, however, is that *before your Cocker is seriously ill,* you and your veterinarian are in agreement when it comes to making the toughest decisions. There are no easy answers because the answers are different for every owner and every dog. The best anyone can do is to try to maintain the highest quality of life possible for their aging Cockers and be thankful for every day they are able to join us.

Chapter Ten

The Field Cocker

The Cocker Spaniel originated as a top-notch hunting dog. In the past 50 years or so, she transitioned from working in the field to becoming a top winning show dog and a loving family pet. She was not bred for her ability to scent birds, quarter, flush, or retrieve—the qualities that are critical for the success of a hunting spaniel. It is believed that a high-quality hunting dog, regardless of breed, is one that is descended from long lines of *proven* "field" dogs.

No one thought that the Cocker had retained much of her hunting instincts. How could she? She had been bred for "type": a classic look that combines a more rounded head, shorter muzzle, flowing coat, and effortless trot. She didn't look much like the early Cockers from the 1800s, and she was distinctly more refined than those in the early 1900s.

And, more important, no one was hunting her competitively. No one was breeding for specific hunting drives. And no one seemed to be actively working with her as a personal hunter or as a competitive field dog. The Cocker, when it came to field work, had literally fallen off the map—and it was assumed that her hunting abilities were lost as well.

In the mid-1980s, an interesting thing happened. Large expanses of land that had been available for hunting with big moving dogs were being swallowed up. Additionally, many folks who were interested in hunting didn't own land and lived in more suburban areas, necessitating a dog that could be a great family pet and a weekend hunter.

The need for a close-working, small spaniel was returning. A group of Cocker fanciers wondered, Were there any Cocker Spaniels remaining that had hunting instincts? And if so, did they have the courage and heart to perform in the field, where the "going" can definitely get rough?

Amazingly, hunters discovered that not only had the little Cocker retained her hunting instincts, but *most* Cockers, regardless of their backgrounds, had significant hunting instincts. Fanciers found that Cockers bred primarily for show, or for performance events (obedience and agility), were able to flush and chase birds *with no training*, and some instinctively retrieved them.

Today, the Cocker is proving her mettle in the field once again. The merry little *hunting* Cocker is alive and well!

Doing What Comes Naturally . . .

To be a good hunting companion, the Cocker Spaniel must have several key drives and abilities. As a flushing spaniel, the Cocker's skill set is quite different from a retriever (who does not play a role in finding birds in cover), or a pointer (who does find birds by quartering but works at such a distance, he is often hunted with the handler on horseback).

The following are the skills that a hunting Cocker Spaniel must possess:

- **A Nose for Birds** The Cocker locates birds by using both ground and air scent. When she is "making game," her body becomes very animated with vigorous, accelerated tail wagging—an embodiment of the term *merry*.
- **Instinct to "Quarter"** The Cocker naturally searches the ground in search of birds in a back-and-forth motion. (With training, the handler can control the width of the sweep.)
- **Close Working and with Deliberate Speed** The Cocker stays within gun range (for a walking hunter), which is usually within 20 to 30 yards (18–27 m) of the hunter.
- **Flushing Skills** When the Cocker is making game, she offers a *momentary hesitation,* in which she uses her ears, eyes, and nose to pinpoint the birds' location, and then boldly flushes the birds from their cover.
- **Ability to Mark** Once the bird(s) take flight, the Cocker Spaniel naturally follows their path, and when a bird is shot, she watches the fall and "marks" the location.
- **Desire to Retrieve** The Cocker is an eager retriever and will go through dense brush and water to retrieve a bird.
- **Strength** The Cocker has been said to have more strength, pound for pound, than many other hunting dogs. She is capable of carrying a rooster pheasant through thick underbrush and berry bushes and leaping over fallen trees, without ever dropping her bird.

Breed Truths

Cockers have been bred for long, lustrous coats. A heavy coat does not do well in the field and tends to be a burr magnet. If you are planning to hunt with your Cocker, you will want to give her an all-over, close clip. Some owners leave a little length (2 inches/5 cm or so), whereas other owners like to take their dogs down to an inch (2.5 cm) or less.

Beginning Training Tactics for Future Hunters

Training for work in the field can begin at any time; however, ideally, a puppy would be started on basic skills immediately. Cockers are soft dogs when it comes to training, and respond best to a confident trainer who uses positive, reward-based training.

For the Cocker, field training is the ultimate in *fun,* and a skilled handler ensures that the little dog never realizes she's being trained and this isn't just a big play session.

The following are some basic areas to begin preparing the young Cocker puppy to work in the field.

Basic Obedience Begin working on the basic commands of *sit, stay,* and *come* (see Chapter 7: "Training and Activities").

Retrieve The most important things to remember when working the *retrieve* are to set your puppy up for success (make it impossible for her to fail) and don't overdo it. To set up the perfect retrieve, sit in a hallway and with your Cocker on a line, throw a bumper a few feet away. She will run after it, pounce on it, and play with it. Encourage her to return to you and play with you. *Don't ask her to give up her prize!* Pat her back and ribs while she holds her prize and say *"What a good girl!"* When you want her to give you her prize, raise your hand under her chin for the release, or wait for her to give it to you on her own. Never try to take it away from her.

Out or Give Command After your puppy has had a chance to really show off her bumper to you, offer her a wonderful treat, something she can't refuse. When she opens her mouth to drop the bumper, link the command *"Out!"* with the action of releasing the bumper. Practice throughout the week with items other than the bumper to help reinforce this command.

Acclimate to the Woods Most Cocker owners do not have access to large expanses of woods and fields in their backyard so try to take your Cocker to wooded parks for walks and light Obedience work. If your puppy doesn't have regular weekly visits to woodsy areas, she may become so excited when you attend a training club practice that you won't accomplish much, if anything.

Gentle Water Introduction Icy cold water and learning by the "sink or swim" method *does not* work with the gentle Cocker. Introduce her to shallow bodies of water, preferably those that are not freezing cold. To entice a reluctant Cocker to get her feet wet, bring along another Cocker (or smaller, friendly dog) that likes to swim. Also, try to find areas of warm water, such as shallow pond a warm, sunny day. Gradual sloping banks with some sand or firm footing help Cockers feel more comfortable entering the water, too.

CAUTION

Limit Retrieve Practice

Top trainers caution owners not to overdo retrieving practice. The goal is to make the young puppy *so* want to play "retrieve" that she can hardly contain herself when she sees you pull out the bumper. This kind of enthusiasm makes for very strong, powerful retrieves.

So, how much is too much practice? Some trainers recommend only two to three tosses a day. Some recommend limiting bumper-tossing sessions to just two to three times *a week*. Regardless of how little you practice the retrieve with your Cocker, it is important that you never get to the point where your Cocker is slow in her retrieves, or worse yet, runs to the bumper and keeps going.

Introduce the Sound of a Blank Do not make the mistake of firing a shotgun directly over your Cocker's head. That will stop her hunting career before she even gets started. The sensitive Cocker needs to hear pistol blanks being fired *at a distance of 50 yards (46 m) or more.* Mark and reward calm behavior (yes, you can use a clicker), and gradually move the sound closer. Another good practice is to clap wood blocks together (at a distance) to call her for dinner every night. This associates a similar loud noise with something good.

Attend a Training Club Training a Cocker Spaniel to work in the field involves a steep learning curve for the first-time owner. Reading training books is helpful, but without a working knowledge of how all the pieces fall together in the field (something invariably goes wrong), trying to train with just book knowledge is extremely difficult. If possible, find a working spaniel club in your area for weekend training sessions, and attend training seminars for flushing spaniels whenever possible. If you can work with an experienced Cocker trainer, or have a mentor you can call to discuss training issues and questions, this will help immensely toward building a solid training foundation and working as a team with your dog in the field.

Working Dog Certificate Program

The American Spaniel Club (ASC) offers two levels of working certificates for the hunting Cocker: a Working Dog (WD) and a Working Dog Excellent (WDX). The tests are not competitive and require a passing score in both land and water segments for the Cocker to receive a certificate.

The Working Certificate program was designed to give Cockers and other flushing spaniels a chance to test their natural hunting skills with nominal training in a noncompetitive environment. Many Cocker owners begin with the certificate program and go on to the American Kennel Club's Hunt Test titling program.

Working Dog (WD)

At this entry level, the Cocker is required to show she can do several things: sit or stay *off-leash* next to or in front of her handler at a starting line, work a field in front of her handler when sent out (by her handler), show a "reasonable" response to voice and/or whistle commands, and when she finds game, flush the birds out of the cover. When the bird is shot, the Cocker must retrieve the bird *without damaging it* and deliver it close (within a few steps) to the handler.

For the water portion, the Cocker can be held on-leash next to the handler. A dead bird is thrown into the water, roughly 10 to 15 yards (9–13.5 m) from the shore. (A shot is fired as the bird is thrown into the water.) The handler is asked to send out his or her Cocker to fetch the bird. The Cocker must enter the water and return the bird close to the handler.

Working Dog Excellent (WDX)

The WDX certificate test is nearly identical to the WD test; however, the Cocker is expected to be more controlled in a few areas. In the land portion, the Cocker is expected to watch the fall of the bird and mark its location *and* deliver the bird to the hand of the handler.

In the water portion of the WDX, the Cocker is expected to be "steady" (off-leash) as she waits beside her owner near the water's edge. The handler may gently restrain her, if needed. Delivery of the bird, as in the land portion, must be to hand.

Hunt Tests

In the early 1980s, the American Kennel Club (AKC) received a request to hold an AKC-sanctioned event called a Spaniel Gun Dog Qualification for the purpose of gauging a dog's natural abilities during demands of actual hunting conditions. A Spaniel Hunting Test Advisory Committee was formed in 1985 to develop an AKC-sanctioned test for spaniels, and three years later, the American Spaniel Club held the first AKC Spaniel Hunting Tests.

The tests provide three levels of titling for spaniels: an entry-level test (Junior Hunter), an intermediate level (Senior Hunter), and an advanced level (Master Hunter). The tests are pass/fail (three passes are required for a title), and each dog is judged against a standard of performance, not each

other. Additionally, in January 2007, a detailed description of each spaniel's unique hunting style was added to the judging standards, so that spaniel breeds with slightly different quartering and flushing styles wouldn't be penalized for varying as a breed from the "norm."

Junior Hunter

At this entry level, the Cocker is required to complete both a land and water segment. On land, the Cocker must find, flush, and retrieve two birds within a general 10-minute time frame. For the water portion, the Cocker must perform a water retrieve of a bird that is roughly 20 to 25 yards (18–22.5 m) into the water. A shot is fired as the bird is tossed into the water. The dog needs four passes or "qualifying legs" for the Junior Hunter title.

Senior Hunter

At the intermediate level, the Cocker must find, flush, and retrieve two birds *to hand* for the land portion. While finding the birds, the Cocker is expected to work efficiently with an intense desire to hunt and cover ground in a distinct pattern at a brisk pace. For the water segment, the Cocker must be "line steady" (swim the straight for the shot bird) and complete a water retrieve of 30 to 35 yards (27–31.5 m) *to hand*.

The Senior Hunter test adds a third requirement: the "hunt dead" test. In this test, a dead bird is placed in cover that is roughly 35 to 40 yards (31.5–36 m) from the dog and handler, but that neither the dog nor handler has seen. The handler then sends out the Cocker to find the downed bird and bring it back *to hand*. The Cocker must qualify five times with a passing score to earn a Senior Hunter title, or if the Cocker has a JH title, she only needs to receive four qualifying legs to receive the SH title.

Master Hunter

The Master Hunter is an amazing dog. Cockers that earn this title are truly outstanding hunting companions. In this advanced level, the Cocker must find, flush, and retrieve two birds to hand on land, and retrieve a bird from water at a range of 40 to 45 yards (36–40.5 m), and deliver it to hand.

Additionally, the master hunter test requires a Cocker to be tested on a blind water retrieve, in which the handler but not the dog sees where the bird falls, roughly 30 to 40 yards (27–36 m) away. The "hunt dead" portion of the test, in which neither handler nor dog sees where the bird has been planted on land, is now performed at a distance of 55 to 60 yards (49.5–54 m). The Cocker, must qualify six times for a MH title; however, if the dog has a SH title, she is only required to receive five qualifying legs.

Fun Facts

Eligible Spaniel Breeds

The following spaniels that can participate in AKC spaniel hunt tests:

- Airedales (as of 7/1/09)
- American Water Spaniels
- Clumber Spaniels
- Cocker Spaniels
- English Cocker Spaniels
- English Springer Spaniels
- Field Spaniels
- Sussex Spaniels
- Welsh Springer Spaniels

Field Trials

Spaniel field trials are sanctioned by the American Kennel Club and are highly competitive. There is no pass/fail here; it is run to win. Dogs are run in braces, not individually (as in hunt tests). And, English Cocker Spaniels and Cocker Spaniels may be run together in what is called a mixed stake. When run with the English Cocker, the Cocker is given no allowances for differences in hunting style, speed, or size.

Classes within a field trial may include "stakes" for Amateur (the handler is an amateur but the dog could be a polished Field Champion); Puppy (six months to two years old); Novice (the spaniel has not placed first through fourth in any regular stake); Novice Handler (the handler has not placed first through fourth in any regular class, and the dog must not have won a class, other than Puppy); and Open (handlers are amateurs or professionals, and the class may be either "Qualified," in which the dog has placed first through fourth before, or "All-Age," which is simply for all dogs over six months).

Points toward a field championship or amateur field championship are accrued by winning first through fourth place within a stake. In addition to earning an amateur field championship (AFC) or a field championship (FC), cockers can compete to win national championship titles.

Resources

Useful Addresses and Contacts

Organizations

American Kennel Club (AKC)
5580 Centerview Drive
Raleigh, NC 27606-3390
(919) 233-9767
www.akc.org
E-mail: info@akc.org

Canadian Kennel Club
200 Ronson Drive, Suite 400
Etobicoke, ON, M9W 5Z9
Canada
(416) 675-5511
www.ckc.ca

The Kennel Club (United Kingdom)
1-5 Clarges Street
Piccadilly, London W1J 8AB
England
0844 463 3980
www.thekennelclub.org.uk

Fédération Cynologique Internationale
FCI Office
Place Albert 1er, 13
B-6530 THUIN
Belgique
Tél: +32.71.59.12.38
www.fci.be

United Kennel Club (UKC)
100 East Kilgore Road
Kalamazoo, MI 49002-5584
(269) 343-9020
www.ukcdogs.com

Cocker Spaniel Clubs (National)
American Spaniel Club, Inc.
P.O. Box 4194
Frankfort, KY 40604-4194
(502) 352-4290
www.asc-cockerspaniel.org
E-mail: ASC.Secretary@gmail.com

Cocker Spaniel Rescue (National)
Note: The ASC and ASCF offer a list of local and regional rescue groups that have been carefully screened for their services.
Heidi Braun, ASC and ASCF
    Rescue Chair
N79W12846 Fond du Lac Avenue
Menomonee Falls, WI 53051
(262) 255-0246
E-mail: TebreezCockers@Juno.Com

Health Organizations

Canine Eye Registration Foundation (CERF)
Veterinary Medical DataBases–
    VMDB/CERF
1717 Philo Road
P.O. Box 3007
Urbana, IL 61803-3007
(217) 693-4800
www.vmdb.org/cerf.html

Canine Health Information Center (CHIC)
2300 E. Nifong Boulevard
Columbia, MO 65201-3806
(573) 442-0418
www.caninehealthinfo.org/chicinfo.html

Orthopedic Foundation for
Animals (OFA)
2300 E. Nifong Boulevard
Columbia, MO 65201-3806
(573) 442-0418
www.offa.org
E-mail: ofa@offa.org

University of Pennsylvania Hip
Improvement Program
(PennHip)
Veterinary Hospital of University
of Pennsylvania
3900 Delancey Street
Philadelphia, PA 19104-6010
(215) 898-4680
www.pennhip.org

Activities/Behavior

Agility
American Kennel Club (AKC)
See listing under "Organizations."

Canine Performance Events, Inc.
(CPE)
P.O. Box 805
South Lyon, MI 48178
www.k9cpe.com
E-mail: cpe@charter.net

North American Dog Agility
Council (NADAC)
P.O. Box 1206
Colbert, OK 74733
www.nadac.com
E-mail: info@nadac.com

United Kennel Club (UKC)
See listing under "Organizations."

United States Dog Agility
Association (USDAA)
P.O. Box 850955
Richardson, TX 75085-0955
(972) 487-2200
www.usdaa.com
E-mail: info@usdaa.com

Animal-Assisted Therapy
The Delta Society
875 124th Avenue NE, Suite 101
Bellevue, WA 98005-2531
(425) 679-5500
www.deltasociety.org
E-mail: info@deltasociety.org

Therapy Dogs International, Inc.
88 Bartley Road
Flanders, NJ 07836
(973) 252-9800
www.tdi-dog.org
E-mail: tdi@gti.net

R.E.A.D.® (Reading Education
Assistance Program)
Intermountain Therapy Animals
P.O. Box 17201
Salt Lake City, UT 84117
(801) 272-3439
www.therapyanimals.org/R.E.A.D.html
E-mail: indo@therapyanimals.org

Behavior/Training
Animal Behavior Society
Indiana University
2611 East 10th Street, #170
Bloomington, IN 47408-2603
(812) 856-5541
www.animalbehavior.org
E-mail: aboffice@indiana.edu

American College of Veterinary
Behaviorists (ACVB)
A listing of all current Diplomates
from the ACVB is found on the organization's website at: *www.dacvb.org*

American Veterinary Medical Association
1931 North Meacham Road, Suite 100
Schaumburg, IL 60173-4360
(800) 248-2862
www.avma.org
E-mail: avmainfo@avma.org

Association of Pet Dog Trainers (APDT)
150 Executive Center Drive, Box 35
Greenville, SC 29615
(800) PET-DOGS
www.apdt.com
E-mail: information@apdt.com

Deaf Dog Education Action Fund
P.O. Box 2840
Oneco, FL 34264-2840
www.deafdogs.org
E-mail: ddeaf@deaf dogs.org

International Association of Canine Professionals
P.O. Box 560156
Montverde, FL 34756-0156
(877) THE-IACP
www.canineprofessionals.com
E-mail: iacpadmin@mindspring.com

National Association of Dog Obedience Instructors
PMB 369
729 Grapevine Highway
Hurst, TX 76054-2085
www.nadoi.org
E-mail: corrsec2@nadoi.org

Canine Good Citizen
See "American Kennel Club."

Conformation
See "American Kennel Club."
See "United Kennel Club."

Field Trials/Hunt Tests
See "American Kennel Club."
See "American Spaniel Club, Inc."

Great Lakes American Cocker Spaniel Hunting Enthusiasts (GLACSHE)
www.GLACSHE.com
E-mail: vdahlke@charter.net

Flyball
North American Flyball Association
1400 West Devon Avenue, #512
Chicago, IL 60660
(800) 318-6312
www.flyball.org
E-mail: flyball@flyball.org

Musical Freestyle
World Canine Freestyle Organization
P.O. Box 350122
Brooklyn, NY 11235
(718) 332-8336
www.worldcaninefreestyle.org
E-mail: wcfodogs@aol.com

Musical Dog Sport Association
515 S. Fry Road
PMB #301
Katy, TX 77450
www.musicaldogsport.org

Obedience
See "American Kennel Club."
See "United Kennel Club."

Rally
See "American Kennel Club."
See "Association of Pet Dog Trainers."

Search and Rescue

National Association for Search and Rescue, Inc.
Education Services Director,
  Janet Adere
(703) 222-6277
www.nasar.org
E-mail: janeta@nasar.org

Tracking

See "American Kennel Club."

Galleries

William Secord Gallery, Inc.
52 East 76th Street
New York, NY 10021
(877) 249-DOGS
www.dogpainting.com

Museum of the Dog
1721 S. Mason Road
St. Louis, MO 63131
(314) 821-3647
www.museumofthedog.org

The National Sporting Library
102 The Plains Road
Middleburg, VA 20118-1335
(540) 687-6542
www.nsl.org

Books

Art

Secord, William. *Dog Painting, 1840–1940, A Social History of the Dog in Art.* Suffolk, England: Antique Collectors' Club, 2003.
————. *A Breed Apart: The Art Collections of the American Kennel Club and The American Kennel Club Museum of The Dog.* Suffolk, England: Antique Collectors' Club, 2001.

Blind Dogs

Levin, RN, Caroline D. *Living with Blind Dogs.* Oregon City, OR: Lantern Publications, 2003.

Deaf Dogs

Becker, Susan Cope. *Living with a Deaf Dog.* Self-published, 1997.
Eaton, Barry. *Hear Hear! A Guide to Training a Deaf Dog.* Self-published, 2005.

Massage

Fox, Michael W. *The Healing Touch for Dogs.* New York: Newmarket Press, 2004.
Tellington-Jones, Linda. *Getting in Touch with Your Dog.* Roxbury, ME: Kenilworth Press, 2006.

Activities

Agility

Canova, Ali, Diane Goodspeed, Joe Canova, and Bruce Curtis. *Agility Training for You and Your Dog: From Backyard Fun to High-Performance Training.* Guilford, CT: Globe Pequot Press, 2008.
Simmons-Moake, Jane. *Agility Training, the Fun Sport for All Dogs.* New York: Howell Book House, 1992.
————. *Excelling at Dog Agility: Book 1: Obstacle Training.* Houston, TX: Flashpaws Productions, 1999.

Animal-Assisted Therapy

Burch, Mary R. *Wanted! Animal Volunteers.* New York: John Wiley & Sons, 2002.
Burch, Mary R., and Aaron Honori Katcher. *Volunteering with Your*

Pet: How to Get Involved in Animal-Assisted Therapy with Any Kind of Pet. New York: John Wiley & Sons, 1996.

Howie, Ann R., Mary Burch, and Ellen Shay. *The Pet Partners Team Training Course: Pets Helping People Manual.* Seattle: Delta Society, 2001.

Canine Good Citizen

Volhard, Jack, and Wendy Volhard. *The Canine Good Citizen: Every Dog Can Be One*, 2nd Edition. New York: John Wiley & Sons, 1997.

Conformation

Coile, D. Caroline. *Show Me! A Dog Showing Primer*, 2nd Edition. Hauppauge, NY: Barron's Educational Series, 2009.

Ronchette, Vicki. *Positive Training for Show Dogs—Building a Relationship for Success.* Wenatchee, WA: Dogwise Publishing, 2007.

Smith, Cheryl S. *The Complete Guide to Showing Your Dog.* New York: Crown, 2001.

Flyball

Olson, Lonnie. *Flyball Racing: The Dog Sport for Everyone.* New York: John Wiley & Sons, 1997.

Parkin, Jacqueline. *Flyball Training—Start to Finish.* Crawford, CO: Alpine Publications, 1998.

Obedience

Anderson, Bobbie. *Building Blocks for Performance.* Crawford, CO: Alpine Publications, 2002.

Bauman, Diane L. *Beyond Basic Dog Training.* New York: John Wiley & Sons, 2003.

Spector, Morgan. *Clicker Training for Obedience: Shaping Top Performance Positively.* Waltham, MA: Sunshine Books, 1999.

Rally

Dearth, Janice. *The Rally Course Book: A Guide to AKC Rally Courses.* Crawford, CO: Alpine Publications, 2004.

Dennison, Pamela S. *Click Your Way to Rally Obedience.* Crawford, CO: Alpine Publications, 2006.

Kramer, Charles "Bud." *Rally-O: The Style of Rally Obedience,* 3rd Edition. Manhattan, KS: Fancee Publications, 2005.

Sawford, Marie. *Rally On.* Guelph, ON, Canada: Dog Sport Media, 2006.

Search and Rescue

American Rescue Dog Association. *Search and Rescue Dogs: Training the K-9 Hero,* 2nd Edition. New York: John Wiley & Sons, 2002.

Hammond, Shirley. *Training the Disaster Search Dog.* Wenatchee, WA: Dogwise Publishing, 2005.

Judah, J. C. *Building a Basic Foundation for Search and Rescue Dog Training.* Morrisville, NC: Lulu Publishing, 2007.

Spaniel Field Training

Craig, Ralph C. *Elementary Spaniel Field Training.* Frankfort, KY: American Spaniel Club, 1947.

Tabaka, Ruth (Editor). *Training Tips for the American Spaniel Club, Spaniel Working Tests and AKC Hunt Tests.* Frankfort, KY: American Spaniel Club, 1999.

Tracking

Krause, Carolyn. *Try Tracking! The Puppy Tracking Primer.* Wenatchee, WA: Dogwise Publishing, 2005.

Sanders, William "Sil." *Enthusiastic Tracking: A Step by Step Training Handbook.* Stanwood, WA: Rime Publications, 1998.

Behavior/Training

General Dog Behavior

Aloff, Brenda. *Canine Body Language, A Photographic Guide.* Wenatchee, WA: Dogwise Publishing, 2005.

Bailey, PhD, Jon S., and Mary R. Burch. *How Dogs Learn.* New York: John Wiley & Sons, 1999.

Coren, Stanley. *How Dogs Think: What the World Looks Like to Them and Why They Act the Way They Do.* New York: Simon & Schuster, 2005.

———. *How to Speak Dog: Mastering the Art of Dog-Human Communication.* New York: Simon & Schuster, 2001.

Donaldson, Jean. *Oh Behave! Dogs from Pavlov to Premack to Pinker.* Wenatchee, WA: Dogwise Publishing, 2008.

Fogle, Bruce. *The Dog's Mind: Understanding Your Dog's Behavior.* New York: John Wiley & Sons, 1990.

McConnell, PhD, Patricia B. *The Other End of the Leash: Why We Do What We Do Around Dogs.* New York: Random House, 2003.

———. *For the Love of a Dog: Understanding Emotion in You and Your Best Friend.* New York: Random House, 2006.

Behavior (Problem)

Donaldson, Jean. *Mine! A Guide to Resource Guarding in Dogs.* San Francisco: Kinship Communications/SF-SPCA, 2002.

Killion, Jane. *When Pigs Fly: Training Success with Impossible Dogs.*

Wenatchee, WA: Dogwise Publishing, 2007.

McConnell, PhD, Patricia B. *I'll Be Home Soon! How to Prevent and Treat Separation Anxiety*. Black Earth, WI: Dog's Best Friend, 2000.

———. *The Cautious Canine: How to Help Dogs Conquer Their Fears*. Black Earth, WI: Dog's Best Friend, 1998.

McConnell, PhD, Patricia B., and Karen B. London, PhD. *The Feisty Fido: Help for the Leash-Aggressive Dog*. Black Earth, WI: Dog's Best Friend, 2003.

Pryor, Karen. *Don't Shoot the Dog! The New Art of Teaching and Training*. Waltham, MA: Sunshine Books, 2006.

Rugass, Turid. *Barking: The Sound of a Language*. Wenatchee, WA: Dogwise Publishing, 2008.

———. *My Dog Pulls. What Do I Do?* Wenatchee, WA: Dogwise Publishing, 2005.

Clicker Training

Book, Mandy, and Cheryl Smith. *Quick Clicks: 40 Fast and Fun Behaviors to Train with a Clicker*. Wenatchee, WA: Dogwise Publishing, 2001.

Pryor, Karen. *Click! Dog Training System*. (Book and clicker.) New York: Metro Books, 2007.

———. *Clicker Training for Dogs*, 4th Edition. Waltham, MA: Sunshine Books, 2005.

Head Halter Training

Fields-Babineau, Miriam. *Dog Training with a Head Halter*. Hauppauge, NY: Barron's Educational Series, 2000.

Housetraining

Kalstone, Shirlee. *How to Housebreak Your Dog in 7 Days*, 2nd Edition. New York: Bantam Books, 2004.

Palika, Liz. *The Pocket Idiot's Guide to Housetraining Your Dog*. New York: Penguin Group (USA), 2007.

Socializing with Dogs

Bennett, Robin, and Susan Briggs. *Off-Leash Dog Play: A Complete Guide to Safety and Fun*. Woodbridge, VA: C&R Publishing, 2008.

McConnell, Patricia B. *Feeling Outnumbered? How to Manage and Enjoy Your Multi-dog Household* (expanded and updated edition). Black Earth, WI: Dog's Best Friend, 2008.

Socializing with People

Long, Lorie. *A Dog Who's Always Welcome: Assistance and Therapy Dog Trainers Teach You How to Socialize and Train Your Companion Dog*. New York: John Wiley & Sons, 2008.

McConnell, Patricia B. *How to Be the Leader of the Pack and Have Your Dog Love You for It!* Black Earth, WI: Dog's Best Friend, 1996.

Trick Training

Haggerty, Captain, and Arthur J. Haggerty. *How to Teach Your Dog to Talk: 125 Easy-to-Learn Tricks Guaranteed to Entertain Both You and Your Pet*. New York: Simon & Schuster, 2000.

Sundance, Kyra. *101 Dog Tricks: Step-by-Step Activities to Engage, Challenge and Bond with Your Dog*. Bloomington, IN: Quarry Books, 2007.

Index

THE TEAM BEHIND THE *TRAIN YOUR DOG* DVD

Host **Nicole Wilde** is a certified Pet Dog Trainer and internationally recognized author and lecturer. Her books include *So You Want to be a Dog Trainer* and *Help for Your Fearful Dog* (Phantom Publishing). In addition to working with dogs, Nicole has been working with wolves and wolf hybrids for over fifteen years and is considered an expert in the field.

Host **Laura Bourhenne** is a Professional Member of the Association of Pet Dog Trainers, and holds a degree in Exotic Animal Training. She has trained many species of animals including several species of primates, birds of prey, and many more. Laura is striving to enrich the lives of pets by training and educating the people they live with.

Director **Leo Zahn** is an award winning director/cinematographer/editor of television commercials, movies, and documentaries. He has directed and edited more than a dozen instructional DVDs through the Picture Company, a subsidiary of Picture Palace, Inc., based in Los Angeles.